Bringing up
Puppy

Everything you need to know
about care and training

Dr Gabriele Lehari

Bringing up Puppy

Everything you need to know
about care and training

Copyright of original edition © 2005 by Cadmos Verlag GmbH,
Im Dorfe 11, 22956 Brunsbek, Germany
Copyright of this edition © 2008 by Cadmos Books, Great Britain
Translation: Andrea Höfling
Cover design and layout: Ravenstein + Partner
Cover photo and pages 2, 3, 8, 11, 92: Christiane Pinnekamp
Editorial: Christopher Long
Printed by: agensketterl Druckerei, Mauerbach

British Library Cataloguing in Publication Data
A catalogue record of this book is available from the British Library.

Printed in Austria

ISBN 978-3-86127-959-4
www.cadmos.co.uk

CONTENTS

INTRODUCTION

One of the most wonderful things for a dog lover is getting to know one's little charge as early as possible, and to take him home while he is still a puppy. I was able to visit all my dogs during the first days of their life. They weren't able to see and hear yet, but a puppy's nose functions straight after birth, able to distinguish and identify individual scents. Thus the smell of my body became one of the first scents that my dogs were able to take in and to confine to memory. Every time I went to visit, my scent was already familiar to the puppy, which probably made it easier for the little mite to deal with the separation from his mother and litter-mates later.

At least my puppies never had any problems settling in – or you may call it being homesick – and they were happy in their new home right from the start. But even if the first time you meet your little pup is at eight weeks old, there is still plenty of time to develop a close relationship. As long as a puppy is still in the imprinting and socialisation phase of his development, we humans are able to play our part in moulding his behaviour and character through our own behaviour and the way we deal with him.

The author with puppy Jerome, aged four weeks.
(Photo: Lehari)

It is simply an unforgettable experience to be part of the development of a creature that is so tiny and helpless to begin with. When the puppy's eyes open after about two weeks, he will be squinting into the sudden glare of his surroundings with a sense of disorientation. At about the same time, the puppy's sensitive ears will also begin to function. Along with the awakening activity of his senses, the puppy will also become increasingly lively and full of enterprising spirit. In the end, you impatiently await the moment when you're going to be able to take your little pup home at the age of eight weeks and after the first immunisation.

Thus begins a beautiful, lovely, but also exceedingly exhausting time. During the first weeks, the little puppy demands your undivided attention. He has to be kept under constant supervision in order to get him housetrained quickly, and to ensure he doesn't do anything that will harm either him or the furniture. The uncompromising affection the little pup displays towards you in return is more than adequate reward. Anybody who has ever had a little puppy fall asleep in their arms, all tired and satisfied after a boisterous playing session and a good feed, will know what I mean.

Whether a harmonious and also enduring relationship with a dog will develop depends to a large degree on human influence. On the one hand, the human needs to know about the puppy's basic needs, and how he can lay the foundations for a long, happy and healthy dog life by ensuring correct nutrition and healthcare. On the other hand, the human should also understand the new family member's language, and know how to make himself understood by the puppy. Communication is a prerequisite for a harmonious relationship, as well as the basic training needs of your canine friend. Never again will a dog learn so quickly and enduringly as in the first months of his life. Therefore this opportunity must not be wasted, but rather be used in best possible way. The major foundations for the dog's further development are laid during this period, and this will be decisive in determining whether or not he will become a faithful and dependable companion.

In this book you will find a wealth of important information and guidance on the selection, purchase, feeding, preventative healthcare, grooming, socialisation and generally dealing with the puppy. Armed with this information, you will be able to enjoy and take advantage of this crucial period, which always passes far too quickly, because your little charge is growing up so fast. The time and affection expended on your dog at this stage will pay off during the dog's entire life.

CHOOSING THE RIGHT BREED

Your decision has been made: you want to acquire a dog, and you want it to be a puppy. All members of the family are in agreement; the distribution of tasks involving the care for the dog has been settled; the costs for equipment, food, vet, insurance, etc., don't present a problem; and you also know a nice responsible person who will look after the dog while you're away on holiday or when you're sick.

You will probably already given some thought to the question of whether you want a pedigree dog or a mixed breed. If you want a pedigree dog, you ought to investigate thoroughly the breeds that interest you, before making up your mind whether it suits you and your requirements. The best way to get an overview over the huge variety of dog breeds that exist is by consulting a relevant book. Reading through such a book, you will soon realise that the number of breeds you might consider as suitable for yourself is being narrowed down rapidly. In the end, only a handful of breeds remain, and these you can investigate more thoroughly. If you have access to the internet, you will quickly find what you're looking for, once you enter the name of a breed into a search engine. Many breeders and pedigree dog associations have very informative websites about their respective breeds. You can ask the Kennel Club for the addresses of breeders who breed your favourite pedigree breed.

Before deciding on a dog, you should investigate the characteristics and needs of his particular breed. Pictured here is a Magyar Vizsla. (Photo: Steimer)

The English bulldog is suitable for less sporty people. (Photo: Lehari)

Breed clubs that are concerned with a breed or a group of similar breeds will be happy to send you brochures about to the various breeds. It would be ideal if you were able experience and observe the dogs in various different situations and circumstances. Ask a number of breeders or owners whether you'll be allowed to visit them in order to get to know the breed a bit better.

Criteria for selecting a breed

• Size

The dog's size should match the size of your home. The smaller the flat and the higher up the building, the smaller the dog ought to be; otherwise he'll constantly bump into walls and furniture. Also on occasion you might have to carry him up the stairs. A house with a garden is, of course, ideal for keeping a dog.

• The texture of the coat

There are dog breeds that don't shed fur (poodles, for example) or that hardly shed any fur (for example, terriers) but that have to be trimmed regularly. Short-haired dogs bring a lot less dirt into the house, and need a lot less grooming than long-haired breeds.

• Character and temperament

Do you want your dog to guard house and home, or do you want him to be a problem-free companion in all of life's circumstances? Do you want him to be sporty and accompany you while out jogging or riding, or do you even want to practise dog sports with him? Or are you rather the easy-going type who would just like to take your dog for quiet walks in the park or in the countryside? There is a right breed for everyone.

• Tendency to bark

The tendency to bark can vary between dogs and is usually dependent on the breed. Small terriers, dachshund, pinscher or spitz for example like to bark relatively frequently. Typical guard dogs give a bark in order to announce strangers; shepherd dogs often bark when they are exited or want to play; molossers, herd protection dogs, greyhounds and many hunting dogs bark less frequently and tend to be very quiet indoors.

Don't accept any of these descriptions on face value, however, especially regarding the qualities of a dog's character, and ask further questions if you are unsure. There is no breed that can be said to be child friendly,

an ideal family dog or particularly intelligent as such. How a dog relates to humans, especially to children, or other animals, primarily depends on how he was socialised and what kind of experiences he's had in the past. Certainly there are some breeds that have a higher stimulus threshold than others, or that have a predisposition to snap or pinch due to their genetic makeup. Some are easily trainable; others, however, have been bred in the past for their ability to work independently. These dogs have characteristics that are often interpreted as stubbornness or pigheadedness, simply because they are harder to train or not trainable at all. One thing that is definitely to be avoided is to go for a particular breed purely on the grounds of appearance. The dog's temperament and his original purpose are far more important criteria, and they should be the deciding factors regarding whether a dog is compatible with you and your personal living situation.

As soon as you have made your final decision regarding the breed, you can begin to look for a suitable breeder. You'll already have an address lists from the internet or the Kennel Club. If you have decided to go for a relatively rare breed, you may have to travel some distance in order to get to a breeder who fulfils your requirements. Also, the next litter may not be planned for a while yet, and you may have to hang on for a few months or longer. With more prolific breeds, your chances of getting a puppy relatively quickly are much greater. But even if getting your ideal dog from a breeder involves some waiting, don't be tempted to turn to shady 'puppy mills' where female dogs are just used as breeding machines, and animals are frequently mated at random, without any concern about inbreeding or genetic diseases. Animals on offer from Eastern European countries usually originate from similar mass breeding enterprises as well. Puppies from these sort of places are often sick, and the vet bills that you'll accumulate will quickly exceed the money you may have saved on the purchase price in the first place.

If you're not particularly concerned about getting a pedigree dog, and you're happy to go for a mixed breed, the search for a suitable dog will look slightly different. There are always mixed breed puppies on offer in newspapers, weeklies or on a notice board at the vet's or at local stores. These are usually the product of an unplanned accidental mating. Often puppies in urgent need of a good home are born at dog homes or at organisations that rescue mistreated animals, or bring them into the country from abroad. Once more, the internet can be very useful for your search, as well.

A mixed breed puppy is a real bag of surprises. All puppies are cute and cuddly, but it is very difficult to predict how they might develop and what they might look like later. Usually you can at least get to see the mother, and from that take a guess how big the dogs may eventually grow to be, and how their character might develop – as long as they are taking after their mother. Of course, it would be ideal to know who the father is, too; at least then you get an idea of from which breed the puppy's ancestors may have descended.

Even though the development of mixed breeds is less predictable, nevertheless they are usually just as good and lovable as their pedigree colleagues. There is no difference regarding care, feeding and training. It is often alleged that mixed breeds are healthier than pedigree dogs, but there is no evidence for that. There is a greater risk of producing unhealthy offspring if the parents have a genetic disorder, rather than two healthy dogs mating, no matter whether they are pedigree or mixed breed. Generally it can be said that large heavy dogs are more likely to develop HD (hip joint displasia) than small to medium-size dogs. However, there are disorders, some

Whether a mixed breed or a pedigree dog, both can develop into good reliable companions. (Photo: Steimer)

of which are genetic, to which small breeds are susceptible, as well, such as a dislocation of the patella. The preventative steps that can be taken regarding these and other diseases will be dealt with in the chapter 'Health and Physical Development'.

A visit to the breeder enables you to get a first-hand idea of how healthy the dogs are and what sort of conditions they are kept in. (Photo: Widmann)

Cropping and docking ban

Please note that in the UK the cropping and docking of dog's ears and tails is illegal.

Exceptions are only made if there are good reasons: for example, the docking of a hunting dog's tail when it is deemed necessary for hunting purposes, or if there is a medical reason. However, every individual case has to be judged on its merit. These exceptions are not allowed to be applied as a principle regarding a whole breed. If you are interested in a breed that used to be subject to cropping or docking, you should make sure that the breeder is complying with the legal requirements. The docking of the tail, which used to be done on puppies only a few days old and often without an anaesthetic, causes considerable pain to these tiny creatures, as sensory-physiological tests have proved.

You should also definitely refrain from importing dogs with docked tails. In some countries, some breeds still have the ears cropped, as well, which can cause a lot of pain to the puppy for a number of weeks. It also greatly limits his freedom of movement, and especially the ability to play and scamper about with other dogs.

Puppies who grow up in a rural setting are usually already used to many environmental stimuli and other animals. (Photo: Widmann)

Once you have found a suitable breeder, arrange a date for a visit. A responsible breeder will suggest himself that you pay him a visit, because he will like to see who is going to buy his puppies. Also, the breeder is often in the best position to judge which puppy would be most compatible with you. While you're there you can also have a good look at the breeding location, whether the dogs look well groomed and healthy, and whether they are well socialised and integrated into the family. Should you find the dogs shut away in some dirty kennel or cubby-hole, if you don't get to see the mother of the puppies at all, or if the dogs are distrustful or even scared of their owner, keep away from this breeder and find another one.

Choosing a mixed breed is usually a completely different ball game. Often the dogs belong to neighbours or friends, and usually grow up well loved and cared for in a family setting. If the dog is from a farm, the conditions there are usually a little more rustic. Often these dogs are well looked after, but may never have seen the inside of a human habitation. Provided they have regular human contact and have not had any negative experiences with people, the chances are that these dogs will be just as good as those who have grown up in a house. From my own experience, I can say that such puppies soon adapt to a civilised lifestyle, and will sometimes even get house-trained more quickly, because they were never able to do their business inside the house. Often they are already used to environmental stimuli such as other animals, tractors, noisy machinery and a whole variety of similar things, which will have a positive and firming effect on their character.

Overview of the different groups of breeds

The variety of dog breeds that exist is enormous. According to estimates, there are 500 different breeds worldwide. The Fédération Cynologique Internationale (FCI), which is the European federation of all pedigree dog associations, recognises 347 dog breeds, although some of these are already extinct. The officially recognised dog breeds, however, also include some very exotic dogs, of whom there are only very few about, possibly only in their country of origin, and which you'll never clap eyes on in this part of the world.

All dog breeds are subdivided into ten groups according to origin and their original utilisation:

Group 1:	**Shepherd dogs and herd dogs**
Group 2:	**Pinscher, schnauzer, Molossoid,**
	Swiss herdsman's dog and others
Group 3:	**Terrier**
Group 4:	**Dachshund**
Group 5:	**Original type dogs,**
	Nordic dogs and spitz
Group 6:	**Laufhund, bloodhound and**
	related breeds
Group 7:	**Vorstehhund**
Group 8:	**Retriever, Stoberhund and waterdog**
Group 9:	**Companion dogs**
Group 10:	**Greyhound**

The texture of the coat, by the way, is not a characteristic of a particular breed. It rather depends on where the dog breed's original habitat used to be, and whether the coat had to provide protection against the weather or injuries. Consequently all Nordic dogs possess a thick coat that is able to withstand even ice and snow, while dogs from deserts or other warm regions always have a very short, smooth coat that, of course, makes them more susceptible to cold weather. Extreme cases are found in Hungarian herd dogs, whose fur will become matted and develop dread locks or slates, and in hairless dogs who are naked except for a single tuft of fur. Because the effort required for grooming a dog's body and coat varies according to the breed-specific texture of the coat, and bearing in mind that this will also affect the amount of dirt created in the house, this factor should also be taken into account when choosing a dog.

Listed below are the most important characteristics of the different breed groups, so that you as a prospective dog owner can gain an overview, and also get an idea which of breed type might be most compatible to you. Nevertheless, as suggested above, before making your decision you should look for more accurate and comprehensive information about the breeds concerned.

Group 1: Shepherd dogs and herd dogs
Original utilisation:
guarding, protecting and herding flocks and herds.
Herding instincts are very pronounced, protective instincts medium to strong, hunting instincts low to medium. They are very eager to work and must be kept occupied mentally, as well as physically, in keeping with the characteristics of their breed, and in order to avoid problem behaviour. They are not for people who like their comforts. As a rule they are easy to train, very leader oriented, and friendly to reserved towards strangers.

The exceptions here are the two wolfhound breeds that have strong hunting instincts and that can only be trained to a certain degree by using a very sensitive approach. They have to be socialised very well, so they don't become timid. They are not for beginners!

The white shepherd dog was only recognised officially by the FCI in 2004, and named white Swiss shepherd. (Photo: Lehari)

Herd protection dogs have pronounced protective instincts and can only be trained by using a very sensitive approach. (Photo: Widmann)

Group 2: Pinscherschnauzer, Molossoid, Swiss herdsman's dogs and others

Original utilisation:
Pinscher and schnauzer – guard and protection dogs;
Molossoids – herd protection dogs, as well as guard and protection dogs;
Swiss herdsman's dogs – herding dogs.
Very strong protective instincts, medium hunting instincts, medium to low herding instincts.

The traditional utility dogs such as Doberman, giant schnauzer, boxer, Rottweiler and mastiffs are very trainable, but need a consistent and assertive pack leader. The other breeds, which were originally bred to guard cattle herds or houses and farms, and to work and act independently, often possess a certain stubbornness and a mind of their own. They can only be trained with a lot of patience and sensitivity, but never to the same extent as, for example, herd dogs.

While smaller breeds are usually livelier and enjoy barking more, the attractiveness of large breeds lies in their calmness and laid-back attitude typical for them. Many of them are reliable guard dogs who will unreservedly defend their humans, if they think it necessary. Most breeds are reserved to mistrustful towards strangers.

Group 3: Terrier

Original utilisation:
hunting fox and badgers; rat terrier, bull terrier.
Strong hunting instincts, medium to strong protective instincts, low herding instincts.

Terriers typically have courage, are self-reliant and are quite sharp. The smaller breeds are very lively, confident and often enjoy barking; they require very consistent training. Representatives of the larger breeds are calm, reliable guardians who are usually very trainable.

The Airedale terrier is a traditional utility dog. The breeding of bull-like terriers is illegal in the UK and keeping them is subject to certain restrictions.

Group 4: Dachshund

Original utilisation:
hunting under ground (hunting fox and badger).
Strong hunting instincts, medium protective instincts, low herding instincts.

For hunting purposes, dachshund had to be self-reliant and courageous. Because they have a mind of their own, they require patient and consistent training. As guardians of house and farm, they also have a certain tendency to bark. There are three different groups (normal, dwarf and rabbit dachshund) and three different coat textures (wire-haired, short-haired and long-haired).

Group 5: Original type dogs, Nordic dogs and spitz

Original utilisation:
hunting dog, sledge dog, herding dog and guard dog, depending on the breed.
These instincts are more or less pronounced in the different breeds depending on their use. Generally, Nordic dogs all have very strong hunting instincts, but are not suitable to be used as guard and protection dogs. European spitz, on the other hand, have hardly any hunting instincts, but are particularly watchful.

Usually medium-sized dogs, they are lively movers and have original characteristics (original type dogs hardly bark at all, bitches are on heat only once a year). Many are difficult to train, especially original type dogs and Asian breeds. With the exception of the spitz, who, as a traditional guard dog, likes to guard house and home, most are not suitable as pure family dogs. Nordic sledge

The basset hound is a laufhund and known for his excellent sense of smell. (Photo: Steimer)

and hunting dogs should be used for sport or hunting, in keeping with their breed characteristics.

Group 6: Laufhund, bloodhound and related breeds
Original utilisation:
laufhund – hunting in a pack in order to track down game and pursue it while barking; bloodhound – works after the shot in order to track down injured game.

Strong hunting instincts, low protective and herding instincts. This is the largest group of breeds mostly comprising hunting dogs who are, on the whole, friendly towards humans. Only very few are kept as family dogs. The beagle has become a friendly family dog without having lost his passion for hunting. He loves to pursue a track, while his high melodious barking can be heard.

This passion for hunting must be taken into account regarding all laufhund. Dalmatian and the Rhodesian ridgebacks can also be counted among this group. Dalmatians have long been popular as family and riding dogs, and are very trainable. The ridgeback, although originally a hunting dog, is now mostly kept as a family dog, at least in our part of the world. He is possessed of a certain stubbornness and has to be trained with a lot of patience and consistence.

The curly coated retriever with his characteristic locks is a representative of a rare retriever breed. (Photo: Widmann))

Group 7: Vorstehhund

Original utilisation:

hunting dogs who will discover game and point it out to the hunter by adopting the typical Vorstehhund position. After the shot, he will retrieve the game. Nowadays these dogs are used as versatile hunting dogs.

Strong hunting instincts, low to medium protective instincts, low herding instincts.

These are lively dogs, generally friendly towards humans, but sometimes they can have a certain sharpness. Most are used as utility dogs for hunting, only very few are kept as pure family dogs. They are very trainable, and closely bond with humans. The strong hunting instincts, however, must be taken into account.

Group 8: Retriever, Stoberhund and waterdog

Original utilisation:

retriever – work after the shot to retrieve the game; Stoberhund – flushing of game/fowl (spaniel, quail dog); waterdogs – retrieval of fowl from the water.

Medium to strong hunting instincts, low to medium protective instincts. Low herding instincts.

Some dogs belonging to this group have developed into very popular family dogs. Many are no longer used for hunting either. They are generally very trainable, and are friendly towards humans. Even though they are often thought of as ideal family dogs, many still have strong hunting instincts, which must be taken into account when going for walks in fields and forests.

The mops is a member of a very old breed and still has a faithful band of devotees. (Photo: Lehari)

All greyhounds, such as the Afghan hound, have a great urge to run. (Photo: Widmann)

Group 9: Companion dogs

Original utilisation:

companion and family dogs, 'toy' dogs.

Medium protective instincts, low hunting and herding instincts.

With a few exceptions, this group of breeds consists of small dog breeds that have been bred without a particular purpose in mind, and that have always served as pure companion dogs. They are usually of a friendly disposition, and can be kept without any problems by people who have little experience with dogs. A typical feature of many of these breeds is a particularly luxurious silky coat that does, however, require regular grooming. Because these dogs have not been bred for a specific purpose, they were not selected for their trainability. For this reason, training them can be a little bothersome. One exception are poodles, who are descended from waterdogs. They are very quick to learn and are therefore very trainable. The smaller companion dogs are particularly suitable for dog-lovers in towns and cities and/or those with limited living space.

Group 10: Greyhound

Original utilisation: hounding.

Strong hunting instincts, medium protective instincts, low herding instincts.

Typical characteristics of greyhounds are a slim body and a great urge to run. Because they have a mind of their own and are self-reliant, their trainability is limited. You can't expect complete subordination. Their attitude towards strangers is friendly to reserved. Greyhounds should have the opportunity to have a regular run on the dog track or to go coursing, or at least to run along a bicycle. As sight hunters, they are not allowed to run free in areas rich in game. The two largest breeds, the Irish wolfhound and the deerhound, are more sedate representatives of this group.

CHOOSING A SUITABLE PUPPY

You have now found the right breeder from whom you want to choose your little pup, be it a pedigree or mixed breed dog. Before making your final choice you should think about whether you prefer a male or a female dog. Some dog-lovers don't mind and would be happy with either. Most have a preference for a particular sex, which isn't necessarily the result of any objective criteria, but simply a good feeling.

Male or female?

In most breeds, the sexes can easily be told apart by look-ing at the dog's build and the shape of the head. The male is generally of a stronger and more muscular build, and has a broader skull than the female. His shoulder height is usually a little greater. Short-haired breeds in partic-ular show off the masculine build, because the smooth coat allows you to see the muscle play more clearly. The slightly more delicately built female appears less athlet-ic, and if she is well fed she can quickly look a little on the plump side. Her more delicate head, and often the fact that her eyes seem gentler, underline the feminine expression.

To a greater or lesser degree, genetic disposition and the individual experiences in their youth will determine how the male dog's confidence develops. Very confident animals usually display a very pronounced territorial behaviour and try to dominate every male dog, even out-side their home territory. If the other male doesn't accept

In puppyhood, the character and physical distinctions between male and female are not very pronounced yet. (Photo: Widmann))

this domination immediately by indicating subordination or by taking flight, or if he displays a similarly confident behaviour, a fight may ensue. If the dogs involved are normal, these fights, which tend to look worse than they actually are, are usually over relatively quickly and don't cause serious injuries. On the other hand, there are also male dogs who are of an extremely placid disposition, especially if they have been socialised well as puppies and as young dogs, who get on well with all other dogs or rather tend to avoid a spat if they can (see below).

The degree of rejection displayed by some male dogs towards their male colleagues can equal the strength of their attraction towards female dogs. Male dogs usually try to court every female around, and will normally put up with any type of behaviour from the lady in question, however unwilling or unfriendly her reaction may be. Male dogs with normal instincts would never attack a female dog. If a male dog encounters a bitch in heat, you won't be able to sweet-talk him away from her. This is because her scent is proving just too seductive, and at the same time she will not reject his advances any more. If there are any bitches in heat in the vicinity, very instinct-driven males should be put on a leash, in order to prevent them looking for a mate by themselves.

Females have generally a less antagonistic and more sanguine attitude towards other dogs than male dogs do. However, it is possible that two bitches will engage in a biting spat with each other. As a rule, though, it can be said that it is rather less common to see female dogs get involved in serious scraps.

Male dogs only start lifting their leg once they have reached sexual maturity. Before that, they squat down in order to urinate. (Photo: Lehari))

A bitch will be on heat every seven to nine months, sometimes even less frequently. This will last for about three weeks, with the receptive period only lasting a few days. While she is on heat, the female's behaviour will change drastically. She will suddenly display a keen interest in male dogs, even if she is normally quite defensive. It is not uncommon that her procreative instincts will make her forget all her good manners, and as a consequence she will try to abscond in order to find a suitable mate. Therefore it is important to keep a particularly close eye on a bitch during this period. While she is in heat, the female has a bloody discharge from her vagina. The amount discharged can vary; some female dogs constantly clean themselves, so that the discharge is barely noticeable, but others can leave bloody stains on carpets and furniture, and you may have to take preventative measures by putting a pair of knickers on her. Male and female dogs can form a very close bond with their human, and they are just as affectionate and as much in need of tender love and care as each other. Female dogs, however, tend to be more sensitive and also easier to lead than males. The male will usually require a slightly more firm and consistent upbringing and training, because he is more likely to try to get his own way. He will, on the other hand, display affectionate behaviour more readily than the female. In addition, he will be much more interested in 'reading' the scent marks of his colleagues, and to leave his 'reply' by way of frequently lifting his leg. The female urinates significantly less often (with the exception of the four weeks directly before and during the heat), so when out walking, you won't be forced to stop at every interesting smelling tree or fence post.

All puppies are cute, which is why it is often hard to make a choice. (Photo: Widmann)

Which puppy to have

The age at which a breeder will be happy to show off the puppies for the first time may vary quite a lot. Some have no problem showing you the puppies after the first few weeks of their lives. Others won't admit any visitors before the puppies are at least four weeks old.

Often breeders already have a long list of orders, which can mean that there are no more puppies available. The breeder will reserve the right to decide which puppy will be assigned to you. This is because he will have observed them on a daily basis, and come to know the character and temperament of each. Consequently, he is in a better position to judge which puppy will be most compatible with you and your needs. Should you have a preference regarding sex or colouration of the coat – if there are any

differences within the litter – then the breeder should, of course, take this into account. In the case of a mixed breed litter, the choice is usually left up to you. Although it is certainly not possible to predict how the little dog will develop after the first weeks of his life, nevertheless you always tend to be spontaneously drawn to a particular puppy, a phenomenon for which there is not always a rational explanation.

Testing a puppy's temperament

To make choosing the right puppy a little easier, a character test can be of some help. This character test will give you a certain amount of insight into the traits of the puppy's character and temperament. You can gain an

By turning him on his back, you are able to test for dominating tendencies, even in a puppy. (Photo: Widmann))

impression of whether a pup is a bit of a dare-devil, timid or well balanced. This character test for puppies should be conducted in an environment unknown to the animals.

1. *First, the level of interest in human strangers will be tested. At this stage you are still a stranger to the puppy after all. How does the puppy react to people who are unknown to him? Put the pup down and walk a few paces away from him. Next try to coax him towards you. If he follows you, it can be assumed that he is more curious and open, rather than timid and shy. The second stage also involves you walking away from him, but this time you don't coax him towards you. Will he wait and stay where he is, and prove to be a cautious little chap, or will he jump up and run after you? The latter can be interpreted as verging on dare-devil behaviour.*

2. *The second test can be used to establish how happy the puppy is to fetch. Simply throw a small toy on the ground a little way away from you, and wait to see if the puppy runs after it, and whether he might even pick it up and carry it around.*

3. *The third test gives you an idea about how dominating the puppy's behaviour is likely to be. For this you take the puppy on your lap, roll him on his side and then have him lie on his back. Now you wait to see how the little chap will react: does he stay calm and friendly, or does he begin to fidget and try to escape from this position? If he displays the latter behaviour, then he has a tendency for dominating behaviour.*

Certainly, this test cannot be the sole basis for your decision about which puppy is the right one for you. It can, however, give you some idea of how you can approach handling a puppy before settling on a purchase, because after all, you both need an opportunity to 'sniff' each other out a little. In the end there will be many other factors contributing significantly to the decision-making process, including, of course, the well-meaning advice of the breeder.

HEALTH AND PHYSICAL DEVELOPMENT

Some breeders offer a veterinary examination just before the pups are handed over, from about eight weeks of age. The vet will check the eyes, ears, teeth, wolf claws (if there are any) and the navel of the dog, if they have been immunised and wormed beforehand. In addition, he will check male dogs to see whether the testicles have properly descended from the abdomen into the scrotum. If the puppies are healthy, they can be picked up by their new owners a few days later.

If your breeder has not carried out this examination already, it will be necessary for you to take the new puppy to the vet straightaway. If the pup has had a check at the breeder's, it will be sufficient if you take him to the vet when it is time for his first follow-up vaccination. Make sure that the visit to the vet is a positive experience for the puppy, so that he won't be scared of the vet in the future. Make the waiting period more agreeable for him by giving him treats and playing with him, and reward him before and after the treatment, even while still in the waiting room, in order to achieve a positive association. Afterwards, take him on a brief walk, before taking him home.

If you take in a puppy who, for whatever reasons, has not had a veterinary check-up yet, and has not been immunised and wormed either, then your first trip should be to the veterinary surgery, where your little charge can be examined and where you can get some thorough advice.

The puppy absorbs important immune substances with the colostric milk, which protect him from infection during the first weeks of his life.
(Photo: Widmann)

Worming and immunisation

Within the first eight hours of their birth, all puppies should have suckled from their mother at least once, in order to absorb some of the colostrum contained in this early milk. This ensures that the youngsters get vital vitamins, minerals and, above all, antibodies, which in the first weeks of life enable their immune system to provide them with sufficient protection against infections. This protection, of course, only refers to the illnesses that the mother herself has had or has been immunised against, and against which she has therefore developed antibodies. The antibodies absorbed with the colostric

milk will reach the puppy's blood via his gut. This will only work during the first two days of life, because afterwards the gut wall will become impenetrable to these gigantic molecules. The duration of this immune protection depends on how many antibodies the puppies have absorbed in this manner. If the mother is healthy and has a good immune system, the protection will last for about eight weeks. The puppies will get their first vaccination only after this time has passed: not before, because the antibodies they have absorbed with their mother's milk and that are otherwise active up to this point, would be

neutralised by the vaccination. Unfortunately, by drinking their mother's milk the newborn puppies can also be infected with roundworm, because they have absorbed the worm larvae while inside the uterus. Roundworm larvae survive in a sort of resting stage inside the mother's body, from where they get transferred to the puppies and develop into mature worms. For this reason, the worming treatment in the second week of life is of paramount importance.

Worming treatment for puppies and young dogs

- From the fourteenth day onwards every fortnight until the eighth or perhaps tenth week of life to fight roundworm.
- At the age of four months, with a broad spectrum worming treatment.
- After that, every three to four months, with a broad spectrum worming treatment.

Immunisation timetable

Disease (abbreviation)	Basic immunisation		Refresher	
	First vaccination	Follow-up	First	Further
Distemper (D)	8th week	12th week	After 12 months	Every 2 years
Infectious canine hepatitis (ICH)	8th week	12th week	After 12 months	Every 2 years
Leptospirosis (L)	8th week	12th week	After 12 months	Once a year
Parvovirosis (P)	8th week	12th week	After 12 months	Once a year
Rabies (R)	12th week	–	After 12 months	Once a year
Parainfluenza (Pi or Para-)*	8th week	12th week	After 6 – 12 months	Once a year
Bordetella (B) *	At least 5 days before risk of infection		After 6 – 10 months, when necessary	
Borreliosis	12th week	16th week	After 6 – 12 months	Every 6–12 months

* Causative agents of the kennel cough

Today it is possible to mark every puppy with a microchip. (Photo: Widmann)

Marking and immunisation passport

In the past, puppies were marked with a tattoo in the ear. Since 2002, they are no longer tattooed, but instead have a microchip implanted under their skin on the left side of the neck by injecting it with a syringe. The tiny chip takes hold inside the connective tissue and becomes encapsulated there. Each microchip contains an individual identification number that can be read with a special scanner. This way a dog can be clearly identified at any time, wherever there is a relevant scanner, whether it is at the vet's surgery, an official authority or at a dog sanctuary.

The identification number is noted in the immunisation passport and can be handed over to be kept at a central registration office (TASSO). There the name and address of the dog's owner are kept on file, so should the dog go missing, it will be possible to identify the dog quickly, once it has been found, and notify its owner.

Since 2004 every dog owner in possession of an EU immunisation passport for his dog is allowed to travel with that dog to any EU member country. Every puppy born in the future will be able to have a microchip and a EU immunisation pass.

Shortly after birth the puppies are still completely helpless and dependent on their mother's care. (Photo: Widmann)

Development of the senses

The dog's physical and mental development are almost complete by the end of his first year of his life. During the first weeks and months in particular, tremendous progress is made in regard to the dog's mental and physical abilities.

When puppies are born, they are completely helpless and completely dependent on their mother's care and nurture. They already have fur, but are still blind and deaf, and their physical mobility is also very limited. Despite this, they are not completely lacking a sense of orientation. Some of their senses already work quite well and guide them to the vital source of nourishment, the teats of their mother, as well as reacting to stimuli necessary for survival, such as warmth, touch and pain. The table on page 34 shows how the senses develop.

Development of a puppy's senses

Sense	Begining of awareness	Maximum sensitivity reached
Touch	Inside the womb	A few days after birth
Temperature	Inside the womb	A few days after birth
Pain	Inside the womb	A few days after birth
Balance	Inside the womb	A few days after birth
Smell via the mouth organ of smell	Well developed straight after birth	At the time of sexual maturity
Smell via nose	Some individual scents a few hours after birth	Increasing effectiveness until the 4th or 5th month
Taste	Inside the womb	A few days after birth
Sight	At about 14 days	At 3 months
Hearing	At about 17 days	At about 3 months

When you take your little darling home at the age of eight weeks, he will have developed from a small, helpless baby dog into a lively, nimble puppy with sharp senses, who is full of mischief and bursting with energy and eagerness to conquer his new world.

Avoid too much too early

A dog is classified as a puppy until about the fourth or fifth month of his life. After that, he is deemed to be a juvenile dog. The exact point at which he can be considered fully grown, mature or adult depends on the breed. As a rule, smaller dog breeds mature faster, both physically and mentally, than large dogs. Most dogs reach their full size after one year, although the development is only complete once all joints and tendons have firmed up, and are supported by a well-developed muscle structure. This point is often not reached until the age of eighteen

months, especially in very large breeds. The permanent moulding of character and temperament of some late developers can take as long as two to three years, as is usually the case with very large breeds, such as many molosser or herd protection dogs. In contrast, many small breeds and many hunting dogs are early developers and reach their mental and physical point of maximum resilience sooner.

A puppy must never be put under excessive mental or physical strain. Confronting him with a large variety of environmental stimuli is certainly helpful with regard to the puppy's development (see next chapter). Too much, however, can be very damaging, such as exposing the little chap to extreme situations or circumstances that may seem menacing to him. You have to find a healthy balance.

There is less danger of exposing your puppy to excessive physical strain. When a little pup doesn't want to walk any further, he will just sit down and not move from

At the beginning, puppies must not be put under too much mental or physical strain. (Photo: Widmann)

the spot. Don't ever force him to keep walking. Simply pick him up and carry him in your arms for a while, or all the way home. Prepare for this eventuality by taking a suitable bag or basket with you, and he will most likely be happy to climb on board as a passenger. If you have an adult dog with you as well, who would naturally like a longer walk, it's especially worth taking a carrier bag with you for the baby dog. This way the puppy can take a little walk whenever he feels like it, and be carried in the bag the for rest of the time.

If you have a very enterprising puppy who will walk with you for half an hour, or even a whole hour with apparent ease, it would be best to put on the brakes a little. A ten-minute walk several times a day is more than

enough for the little pup. As he gets older, you can slowly increase the duration of the walks.

Likewise puppies should not have to climb stairs, if it can be avoided at all. As long as the size of the dog and the condition of your back permit it, you ought to carry the puppy up and down the stairs. Too much stair-climbing before the puppy's joints are fully matured can damage them. Even though puppies of larger breeds will be able to climb stairs by themselves relatively early, it is still important to remember that they, too, should be carried as long as possible. Of course, at some point they will have reached a weight at which this will no longer be possible.

The puppy needs a suitable object on which to chew so he doesn't chew other things. (Photo: Widmann)

Dental development

A puppy is born without teeth. The milk teeth break through between the third and the sixth week of life. The pointy little teeth can be quite painful, which you will notice soon enough when playing with the little pup. The mother, too, while she is still suckling her puppies, will also suffer from the impact of their tiny teeth, and her teats may soon be worse for wear. Puppies have a set of twenty-eight milk teeth. The rear molars are missing. At about the fifth month, sometimes earlier, the milk teeth begin to fall out and make way for the permanent teeth. The complete set is comprised of twenty teeth in the upper jaw and twenty-two in the lower jaw.

During the change of teeth, the puppy's urge to gnaw is particularly pronounced. Chair legs, carpets, shoes: nothing is safe from those tiny teeth. Give your pup enough chewable objects during this time, in order to allow him to satisfy his urge to chew. When you leave him on his own, make sure you limit the area accessible to him, in order to prevent him from doing too much damage. The best solution, of course, is to get him used to a dog crate, where he can slumber happily until his human has time for him again.

During the change of teeth it is advisable to refrain from tug-of-war games involving pieces of cloth, soft toys or toy rope, because this may cause teeth to be pulled out with force. As the permanent teeth break through, if it becomes apparent that there may be a problem with tooth alignment, it is possible to correct this yourself by frequently and regularly massaging the tooth in question. This can be done by applying gentle pressure to the affected area as often as possible, for a few seconds or a minute, in frequent intervals and spread over the whole day. By doing this you may be able avoid extensive orthodontic treatment in the future.

THE PUPPY MOVES IN

Preparation and basic equipment

Before your new house-mate finally moves in, you have to make certain safety arrangements in house and garden, in order to eliminate any hazards that may cause injury to the little chap. Check that all safeguards listed have been put into place, and also check that your house and garden doesn't harbour any further potential risks from which the puppy has to be protected.

Check that:
- *The garden has a secure fence around it,*
  as does the pond (if there is one).
- *All access to stairs (up and down) has been*
  secured with stair guards (for example, a gate).
- *Low sockets are secured with child safety devices.*
- *There are no electric cables accessible to*
  the puppy, which he might gnaw.
- *Toxic substances, such as weed killer or other*
  chemicals, have been put away safely,
  out of the puppy's reach.
- *All indoor plants have been placed outside*
  the puppy's reach, because some of them
  are poisonous to dogs.
- *If necessary, any other pets living in house or*
  garden have been put into puppy-proof cages
  or conservatories.

Puppies like to gnaw on everything. That's why potentially poisonous plants should be placed out of their reach. (Photo: Widmann)

When you bring a puppy into the house, bear in mind that during the first few weeks the little chap has to be watched 24 hours a day. If you are working, please try to arrange to take some time off work, enabling you to spend quality time with your puppy. This will give him an opportunity to familiarise himself with his new 'pack', as well as his new home. In addition, he will be able to learn his first lessons during this time. If it is not possible for you to arrange for someone to be at home at all times for several weeks, then maybe you should decide not to have a puppy, but get an older dog instead.

All the necessary utensils that are part of the basic equipment for a dog have to be in place and ready for the puppy's arrival. These include:

- *Two bowls (one for fresh drinking water, one for food)*
- *A blanket and/or a basket*
- *A collar, as well as a harness or leash*
- *Enough food for the first few days*
- *Nibbles/treats*
- *Grooming utensils (comb, brush, etc.)*
- *Suitable puppy toys (squeaking toys made from latex, toy ropes, soft toys that don't have dangerous metal or plastic parts and similar items)*

A warm, soft sleeping place is important for a puppy. (Photo: Widmann)

Before the puppy moves in you have to work out where the little chap is going to sleep at night, and where he will be allowed to spend the greater part of the day. It would be best to have the puppy sleep in your bedroom, at least during the first few weeks. For one thing, this strengthens the bond between human and puppy, and also in your 'private sphere' the smells tend to be exclusively those of your own family, as opposed to the living area, where the family's own scent is drowned out by smells brought in by visitors. In addition, it enables the puppy to attract your attention when he needs to go outside, or if he has any other problem.

Later, when the dog is house-trained and sleeping through the night, you can, if you wish, gradually get him to get used to a new spot outside the bedroom by moving his blanket or basket a little further towards his final designated sleeping place every day.

Every member of the family should be in agreement on whether the puppy will be allowed to roam free everywhere inside the house, or if he is only allowed in certain rooms. In any case, the puppy has to be allocated a warm, draught-free spot that he can use as a refuge, something he may occasionally even be forced to do if, for example, you have visitors who are scared of dogs, even puppies. Under no circumstances must the puppy be allowed to lie in a humid and/or cold place, because his little body is still very susceptible.

First of all, the puppy has to have an opportunity to inspect his new surroundings. (Photo: Steimer)

Transfer and settling in

You should collect your new house-mate in person. Under no circumstances must the puppy be delivered like a parcel. On his own, in a dark container and confronted with a huge amount of strange noises and smells, the little chap will be scared and become completely disturbed.

Before you start on your way home the breeder will hand all the required papers over to you. These include:

- *A bill of sale signed by both parties and that will also state the payment details. Many breeders include an obligation for the purchaser to have the dog x-rayed later to establish whether they have HD (and, if applicable, elbow displasia (ED)), because the results could be very important for future breeding. Often, a previously agreed sum of the purchase price will be returned upon sending the x-ray results to the breeder.*
- *A health record booklet including information about immunisation and worming already carried out.*
- *If the breeder is registered with the Kennel Club, the puppy and his litter will have been registered with the Club, and have a registration certificate (giving six weeks, free pet insurance) and a puppy contract.*
- *A puppy diet and care sheet, as well as some food for the first few days.*

If you are collecting a mixed breed puppy, you should at least receive an immunisation passport and a receipt of the worming treatments carried out.

It would be best take a companion with you when you go to collect the puppy, so one person can drive without being distracted while the other take care of the puppy. You should take collar and leash for a potential stop-over, a box or basket with a blanket, as well as a bowl and drinking water, so the puppy's needs are well catered for, especially on a longer trip.

The best time to collect the puppy is in the morning. This way you will have more time left to spend at home with your new puppy. It would be terrible for the puppy, if his new 'pack' were to turn in for the night shortly after he has arrived at his new home. It is much better if he is able familiarise himself with his new surroundings, and play and cuddle with his new human 'pack', before falling asleep, tired and overwhelmed, for the first time far away from his mother and litter-mates.

The puppy should not be fed shortly before the trip, or he might feel sick during the car ride. The passenger can take the puppy either on his lap or put him in a box (with a blanket laid out inside), or in a basket next to them on the back seat, in order to be able to keep him calm and relaxed. If you have no choice but to collect your puppy on your own, you'll have to put him inside a secure transport crate to prevent him from jumping around inside the car.

Avoid having visitors call just after the puppy has arrived. The little chap will be thrown off balance already due to the separation from his mother and litter-mates, as well as by the exiting car ride. Things would get even more stressful for him if there was a lot going on in the house straightaway. In the beginning, he needs a calm atmosphere to allow him to get used to his new surroundings and his new pack.

Once at home, the puppy should be given a chance relieve himself in a preordained spot. After he has done his business, he should get a big praise. Be careful not to praise him in mid-action though, otherwise he may stop and do the rest inside the house. Once he has relieved himself, he'll be allowed inside in order to start exploring part of his new home. Talk to him a lot in an affectionate tone of voice and play with him. After a while, he ought to be taken back outside again to give him the opportunity to relieve himself once more. Afterwards he should be given his first meal inside the house.

After another trip outside to relieve himself, he will probably be full-up and tired and ready for a nap. Once he wakes, he'll have to be taken outside again immediately.

If at all possible, for the first day and night all the daily routines should be carried out by the same person. This will enable the puppy to develop a close bond and trust quite quickly, which he can then slowly extend to all the other family members.

Having spent the first hours together successfully playing, cuddling, watching, feeding, going out, etc., you're now looking forward to the first night. It is advisable to have the puppy sleep close to his humans. Should this not be possible because of lack of space, initially one family member should spend the night with the puppy. This is the only way to make sure that someone will notice when the puppy is calling. If he becomes anxious, a little cuddle and quiet coaxing will calm him quickly. This will make the separation from his mother and litter-mates less difficult. He will feel less abandoned, and learn to trust his new surroundings and, of course, you, and he will start sleeping through the night much more quickly.

By spending a lot of quality with your puppy at the beginning, you're helping him to overcome the separation from his mother and litter-mates. (Photo: Steimer)

However cute the new puppy may be, he will have to learn from day one what he is and what he is not allowed to do in his new home. If you don't want the dog to enter certain parts of the house, or do certain things, by the time he is fully grown, you will have to make this clear to the puppy. How is the adult dog supposed to understand why all of a sudden he isn't allowed to do things any more that were permitted when he was little? Clear rules right from the start provide certainty and also security.

House-training

One of the most important subjects that will keep the new puppy owner particularly busy in the first few weeks, and that will also determine his daily routine, is house-training. If the puppy was kept inside the house at the breeder's, he will probably have learnt the first lessons already. But even if this is not the case, you can quickly teach your puppy to be house-trained, if you observe certain things, such as keeping an eye on him for twenty-four hours a day at the beginning.

Show the puppy a suitable spot where he can do his business right at the start, and he will always go to the same spot in the future.
(Photo: Widmann)

It is in a puppy's nature not to soil his nest any more once he has started to explore his surroundings. Puppies will move away from the nest, i.e., box or basket, in order to defecate and urinate. Once the puppy has moved in with you, you have to teach him to do his business outside the house, and that he will have to attract attention when he needs to relieve himself. This is not exactly easy at the beginning, however, because the puppy isn't able to control his sphincter very well before the age of three months. This is why he isn't able to hold back for longer periods of time.

The life of a puppy consists mainly of three things: sleeping, eating and playing. After each of these activities, a puppy needs to be able to relieve himself. Every time the puppy wakes up, has eaten or played for a while, he should be taken outside where he should be persuaded to relieve himself, if possible by using the same encouraging words on each occasion. As soon as he has

A puppy will normally be house-trained within three to four months, and call when he needs to go. (Photo: Steimer)

produced a little puddle or a little pile, he ought to be praised enthusiastically. Soon he will understand what you're asking of him, and he will relieve himself quickly upon hearing your words of encouragement. At this time, you can also teach him to only do his business in a particular spot. If the puppy has always been brought to a certain corner in the garden or to a bushy area, he will later prefer similar areas, and only use the pavement or other areas without vegetation for his toilet in an emergency.

Even if you think you have taken the puppy outside often enough, you may still find him occasionally run-

ning around searching and perhaps whimpering a little only a short while after his last trip outside. Don't ignore this behaviour and take him outside straightaway. When a little puppy who isn't able to control his bodily functions properly yet gets exited or pleased, it may happen on occasion that this will stimulate or increase his bowel movements.

A garden, of course, is a valuable asset for house training, because you can take the puppy outside for a toilet any time day or night. If you have no access to a garden, you simply have to be prepared to take your little charge out into the street innumerable times during the first few weeks – and at the beginning during the night, too. If you have to use the stairs for this, you should carry the puppy in order to avoid a little mishap on the way, and above all to prevent damage to the puppy's spine and joints.

Most puppies would not voluntarily soil their own space. That's why the puppy's sleeping area should be closed in as far as possible, to ensure that he will call if he needs to go outside. This means closing doors to other rooms, putting the puppy inside a blanket lined box with an open top, or fencing in the sleeping area with a board. Alternatively, you could also put the puppy inside a transport crate with bars during the night, which you can keep next to your bed. We humans often associate the dog crate as some sort of a prison, but a puppy tends to feel secure and relaxed while inside, and in the future he may even like to use his crate as a refuge, if he had been used to sleeping there at the beginning. If this is the case, you can even occasionally leave him in the crate when you need to leave him alone for a short time, or during his nap or while he is gnawing on a chew bone. Make sure that you buy a big enough transport crate so you dog will still fit inside once he is fully grown.

If you are not able simply to pop into your own garden at nights, have a jogging suit or something similar ready, so you can quickly get dressed to go outside. When the little chap calls for attention, it usually tends to be very urgent. A torch would also be useful if the lawn or the garden are not very brightly lit. Should the puppy just want to be played with, don't let him have his way; the night is for sleeping and not for playing!

If you take thorough care of the puppy during the first few weeks, watching him closely and bringing him outside often enough, he will quickly learn to be house-trained. If a little mishap does happen, despite every-

thing, don't ever punish him; usually it is only your own inattention that is to blame anyway. Instead, take him outside once more, and give him extra praise if he does his business. What is particularly wrong and also completely ineffective is the hideous tradition of pushing the puppy's nose into the evidence of his 'misdeed'. This will just make him feel insecure, and it won't get him house-trained any quicker.

The last thing before going to bed should be a trip outside with the puppy. Once he sleeps through the night until morning without having to go outside, you can start getting him used to sleeping in his designated spot.

As soon as the puppy has understood that he has to go outside in order to relieve himself, and as soon as he can control his bladder and bowels more effectively, he will call when he needs to go. From this point onwards, you can gradually increase the intervals between the trips outside. After three months, the puppy should be house-trained, although some puppies may possibly take a little longer.

The regular grooming of the coat can already be practised on the puppy — disguised as play. (Photo: Steimer)

Grooming

Puppies don't normally need much grooming. However, it would be useful to familiarise him early with all the necessary measures that he will have to endure in later life. In particular, dogs whose breeds need to have their coat trimmed or sheared regularly should get used to this procedure as early as possible.

These are a few things you can practise with the puppy already:
- *Daily control and cleaning of teeth, eyes and ears*
- *Grooming of the coat (brushing, combing, curry combing)*
- *Clipping of claws (pretend)*
- *Cleaning paws and coat (practise during fine weather)*
- *Taking objects and food out of the dog's mouth*

- *Checking the body for parasites, injuries, etc.*
- *Taking the temperature from the rectum (This should really be practised while the puppy is healthy. Otherwise, once the puppy is ill and you're nervous, this procedure can be very laborious.)*
- *Giving medicines*

If you plan to enter dog shows with your dog later, you can get the puppy used to some ring training already. This doesn't just involve the walking on the leash in the correct rhythm, but also the correct posture and presentation. In addition, the dog has to be prepared to let the judge check his teeth and testicles as well. If this can be practised while he's still little, it will not represent a problem later on.

FEEDING

Up to the third week of life, puppies exclusively drink their mother's milk. After that, extra feeding can be introduced slowly. From the fifth or sixth week onwards, the puppies will be weaned, so that they can be fed on puppy food without any problems after they have been collected by their new owners at the age of eight weeks.

The best option is to give dried food, which can be weighed according to the manufacturer's recommendations to match the puppy's weight precisely. In the first few days, the dried food should be soaked in a little lukewarm water. Once the puppies have got used to this, the dried food can be offered without previous soaking. When you feed dried food, please bear in mind that the food will swell up inside the puppy's tummy. Even if the weighed portion does look rather small, it will certainly be sufficient.

The puppies should be given the opportunity to eat as much as they need. You have to make sure that each puppy gets a sufficient amount of food, because often smaller or weaker ones will be pushed to one side by their brothers and sisters. The food should be spread out over four or five meals.

Make sure that the dog also has access to clean drinking water at all times.

Try to feed your puppy the same type of food as he was previously given by the breeder. (Photo: Widmann)

Up to the third month, the puppy should still be given four to five meals a day. After that, the number of meals can be reduced to three, and after six months to two meals per day. When the dog has reached one year of age, one main meal will be sufficient, provided he is getting dog biscuits and other treats offered to him during the rest of the day. For large dog breeds, it is best to stick to two meals per day, in order to prevent them from overfilling their stomachs; large dogs have a greater predisposition to twist their stomachs.

It used to be thought that a puppy or a young dog ought to be given additional vitamin and mineral supplements to ensure a healthy development, or that he ought to eat a lot of soft bones or gristle in order to ensure a sufficient intake of calcium and phosphorus. This is not the case, provided a special puppy food preparation is given. Supplemental vitamins and minerals offer no advantage to the dog. On the contrary, they can even damage the dog's health. Feeding too much supplemental calcium, for example, can influence the absorption of other important substances, such as phosphorous, zinc or copper in a negative way, resulting indirectly in malnutrition.

Large, tall breeds in particular should not be overfed as young dogs, because any over-rapid growth can cause or promote skeletal diseases, such as hip joint displasia (HD). Small breeds should have reached approximately seventy-five to eighty per cent of their final weight by the age of six months. In contrast, large breeds should not weigh in at more than sixty to sixty-five per cent of their final weight. The larger the dog is expected to grow, the smaller his rations should be in his first year.

How many meals does a puppy need?

- At six to twelve weeks – four meals
- At three to six months – three meals
- From seven months onwards – two meals

Many puppies initially have problems feeding because of the absence of their greedy litter-mates. Don't get distracted by this behaviour, and don't be tempted into offering him different and seemingly better food. If the puppy doesn't eat properly, just put the meal in the fridge (not necessary with dried food) and he'll be presented with it at his next meal time. Never feed the cold food straight from the fridge!

You must never feed him raw pork, because it may cause the Aujeszky-disease, which is always lethal. Bones are not a suitable food either, because they can cause a condition called cement faeces, which have to be removed by the vet via a painful procedure.

IMPRINTING AND SOCIALISATION

Books about dogs often refer to an imprinting phase to which puppies are subject, although the data given for the duration of this phase varies. The reason for this is that when applied to puppies in a more commonly used sense, imprinting actually means socialisation, but biologically speaking, imprinting means a learning process where the ability to learn is limited to a usually short, sensitive phase. This learning process only takes place after it has been caused by a definitive trigger signal, and the learning results are irreversible. If this imprinting phase is allowed to pass without making use of it, as a rule this will result in disturbed behaviour later on. The best-known examples for this are goslings who are imprinted to follow their mother (or surrogate mother) around, and the sexual imprinting of birds to mate within their own species.

This explanation clarifies that imprinting, when used in regard to puppies, actually means a form of socialisation during which the puppy familiarises himself with various environmental stimuli, humans and other animals. These learning processes don't just relate to one trigger signal, but to a whole host of different signals. The period of time, during which the puppy is most receptive to this socialisation, and also able to learn rapidly and enduringly, lasts from his fourth to his twelfth week of life. This doesn't mean that the puppy won't be able to progress and learn from any further experiences after that, only that it will never be as easy for him as during this early phase.

From the fourth week onwards, the development of the puppy's sense organs is almost complete, and he will be confronted with an ever-increasing amount of environmental stimuli. This kicks off his brain development full steam. The learning processes also happen on a physical level inside the nervous system. If the sensual stimulation is absent during this phase, the development of

The puppy will never again learn as rapidly and as enduringly as between his fourth and his twelfth week of life. For this reason, this time should be used sensibly. (Photo: Steimer)

relevant nerve connections will be retarded, a deficit that can never be made up again for the rest of the dog's life. The development of the brain is promoted by experiencing a great variety of sensual impressions and challenges, and the more efficient the brain is working, the better the dog is prepared for everyday life.

During the short period up to the twelfth week, the puppies are bright, curious and uninhibited. Fear or distrust of strangers are yet unknown to them. They take everything that happens to them in their stride. Having said this, they should not, of course, be exposed to extreme stimuli

that may startle them too much or even cause them pain. As they get older, the little chaps become more and more distrustful, occasionally displaying avoidance behaviour. This is completely normal, because their curiosity is now joined by feelings of anxiety. At about thirteen weeks, their fear of strangers outweighs their curiosity. If the puppies are exposed to a variety of environmental stimuli only after this point, the learning process will take a lot longer. Of course, the dog can continue to have experiences and carry on learning – all his life – but his environmental confidence will already have suffered.

Up to the twelfth week of life, the puppy is curious and uninhibited, running through a tube tunnel is no problem at all. (Photo: Widmann)

Because the sensitive phase already begins as early as the age of four weeks, the breeder carries a huge responsibility. Until the handover of the puppies, it is mainly up to him whether the puppies will develop a close relationship with humans, and will be able to deal with a host of environmental stimuli. He has to make sure that the puppies come into contact with a variety of human beings (young and old, women and men) and that this is a positive experience for them. They should be stroked every day and be fed by hand. An interesting adventure playground set up inside the house or outdoors, depending on the time of the year, will help educate the puppies' senses, and at the same time improve their physical abilities. It should contain a variety of toys, cardboard boxes or tunnels for crawling inside, climbing features made from wood or stone, and many other such items.

After the puppy has been handed over, the new owner takes on the responsible task for continuing to socialise the little chap well. As a brand-new puppy owner, you can contribute tremendously to exploiting this sensitive socialisation phase to the best advantage. As a reward,

Only by dealing with other dogs can the puppy learn to interpret the different signals properly. (Photo: Steimer)

you will get to have a dog with a firm character and temperament, who will confidently accompany you in any kind of situation. Familiarise him gently with a great variety of different environmental stimuli and situations. For instance, at the beginning take your puppy for a walk in a quiet street – of course, on a leash – where you're likely to encounter other people and occasionally a car, motorbike or bicycle. Next, choose a slightly busier street for your walks, and also occasionally begin to take the puppy with you to town. After a few weeks, the puppy will be happy to trot along beside you in a relaxed manner at a railway station, airport or funfair, as well. In this way, you can familiarise him increasingly with a great

variety of different situations. Don't forget to show him a large variety of animals in good time as well, such as cows, horses, sheep, goats, small animals and fowl, in order to teach him straightaway that there's no need to be scared of them, and also that he is not allowed to chase them.

If the puppy encounters a situation in which he feels insecure, don't relieve him of all his woes straightaway. He will have to learn how to deal with an unfamiliar situation and occasionally solve a problem on his own as well. Allow him to try out which kind of behaviour is most appropriate for which kind of situation: explore, sniff, run away, freeze, submit or threaten. If he has experience of how certain situations are to be dealt with, his confidence will grow. As a result, he will also become more relaxed, and able to interpret such behaviour better in other dogs, which is especially important with regard to threatening and aggressive behaviour. A puppy who has never experienced what it means to be threatened and who has always been protected and cocooned, may later, once he is no longer a puppy, misunderstand or misinterpret important threatening gestures from his fellow canines. He may get into a lot of trouble as a result.

When travelling with your puppy during this sensitive socialisation phase, you should behave in a relatively unconcerned manner. Don't make a big deal out of everyday situations that may possibly frighten the little chap. The puppy will take his cue from you, and if you are signalling that everything is fine, he will calm down quickly and no longer show any fear. Whatever you do, don't pity him, or take him in your arms and comfort him. This would only reinforce his anxiety and insecurity even more. You have to be the superior boss of the pack, who inspires confidence in the puppy and gives him security.

The puppy group

Opinion is divided on at what age a puppy should join a socialisation class or puppy group. Some believe that a puppy should be in possession of a complete set of immunisations beforehand, which isn't the case until the age of twelve weeks. By this time, however, the sensitive phase in which the puppy is able to acquire enduring knowledge and is best equipped to deal with different environmental stimuli has already passed.

I am rather in favour of visiting a puppy group as early as possible, because the risk of infection is much higher during a daily walk or a visit to the veterinary surgery than in a group of healthy puppies who have already had their first vaccination.

The puppy should be given the opportunity to take part in his first socialisation class as early as possible, within a few days after having been separated from his mother and litter-mates. The contact with other puppies will help him to overcome the separation from his family more quickly. He will not only become more fixated on his human, but also learn and develop species-typical behaviour from social contact with other dogs. With the right guidance, the puppy will become confident but not too dominating, placid but not anxious, and moreover, a dependable partner.

During socialisation classes, puppies don't just have the opportunity to play with other puppies with gusto, which promotes the development of their social behaviour, but they also learn quickly and intensively, so the first lessons of dog training, such as 'come', 'sit', 'down', 'stay', as well as walking on a leash, can already be practised with them. In addition, they are being familiarised with the greatest possible number of everyday situations as well. This may include a bus ride, a trip to town plus a visit to a department store, the exploration of varied

Visiting a puppy group plays an important part in the socialisation process. (Photo: Widmann)

and interesting terrain, or the first swimming lessons. The humans will also learn the theory and the practice of how to behave properly, and how to continue practising with their little charges at home.

The puppy socialisation classes usually admit puppies between the ages of eight and sixteen weeks. There are weekly meetings being held over a period of six to eight weeks. As mentioned before, because the particularly sensitive phase lasts until the twelfth week of a puppy's life, the puppies should take part in these puppy socialisation classes as early as possible. Anyone interested can also visit a class for juvenile dogs afterwards, during which less emphasis is put on play and more on seri-

ous training exercises for the youngsters. Often this can provide the foundation for becoming support and assistance dogs.

At most dog training schools where puppy socialisation classes are offered, agility equipment is also available, such as tube tunnel, plank walk and seesaw, to which the puppies can carefully be introduced even at this early stage. Please make sure, however, that the puppies are always supervised when they are running over or under these structures, especially when these are raised off the ground, because puppies tend to be enthusiastic and clumsy, and fall off such a structure can cause your pup to hurt himself seriously, and he may end up

When a puppy is being introduced to various obstacles, there should always be a second person making sure the little chap doesn't fall off. (Photo: Lehari)

being forever scared of you afterwards. Only lead him across the plank walk and seesaw while on the leash. In addition, it would be best to have a second person on the other side to make sure the puppy doesn't tumble down. Jumps of any kind are still taboo for the little chap, no matter how enthusiastic he may be. A dog should not start to practise jumping before the age of eighteen months. The larger the breed, the later the dog should start to jump.

At this point, it should be noted that all collars should be removed from the puppies for these playing sessions, because they may cause injury. Later on, when the dogs have grown up, they should also be allowed to play with other dogs without a collar, if at all possible, because occasionally they might get their claws or teeth caught in the collar of their playmate and hurt themselves.

Find out from your breeder, your local dog club or pedigree association where puppy socialisation classes are being offered. Sometimes this information is also available from daily newspapers, dog magazines or the internet, or perhaps your vet or the local RSPCA may be able to advise you. Be sure to enrol for these sociali-sation classes in time, and make the time to attend each of these meetings, because they are so important for your puppy's development.

Bouncing about with other dogs is what makes a walk into a great adventure. (Photo: Lehari)

Going for a walk

At the beginning, the puppy should not be taken on walks more than ten minutes long. With increasing age, the length and duration of the walks can gradually be increased. The main objective of the walk is to give the puppy an opportunity to explore his surroundings, to get to know different terrains, and to be exposed to a variety of acoustic and visual stimuli.

You will usually meet other dog owners on these daily walks. If you always walk in the same area, you will soon get to know the other dogs, and work out with whom you can let your puppy play without worry. Playing with his peers is tremendously important for every puppy, in order to develop his social behaviour and physical skills.

If a dog owner with a dog on a leash is coming from the other direction, put your puppy on his leash too, and either ask the other dog owner, if your dogs are allowed

to play with each other, or just walk past them while distracting your puppy's attention with a toy or a treat. If you come across a dog who is running free without a leash, you can also allow your puppy to scamper about and play with him, if he wants to. There should definitely be no rollicking about at all while on the leash.

Make the daily walks interesting by involving the puppy in exiting games, such as climbing or jumping over tree trunks, playing fetch, crawling under something, hide and seek – the possibilities are endless. These shared experiences enhance the relationship between human and dog, and the puppy's development.

You, rather than your puppy, ought to be aware of what or who is coming. If danger is on the horizon, recall him in time and put him on his leash. This way he can observe cars, cyclists, motorbikes and joggers in peace, and in time he'll learn not to be scared of them or run after them, as the case may be. Don't overwhelm your puppy with too many stimuli at once, but instead let him get used

If puppies are too rude towards an adult dog, they are often put in their place. (Photo: Lehari)

to new situations step by step, first in the great outdoors, then in streets situated in calm areas, later in pedestrian precincts, railway stations, airports, etc. Especially while out in urban areas, as well as public spaces and buildings, you should not forget to take a little bag with you to pick up potential souvenirs left behind by the puppy, because little mishaps are bound to happen.

The myth of protective behaviour towards puppies

It is often alleged that puppies enjoy unlimited puppy protection, i.e., they will be able to behave badly towards older dogs without the risk of reprisals. This is correct only to a degree. In a wolf pack there is indeed such a thing as protective behaviour towards puppies. This is because almost all pack members are related to each other, and for many species it is true that blood relations

are not attacked, or are even protected, in order to preserve one's own genes. But if adolescent pups behave too badly towards adult pack members, these won't always wear kid gloves when teaching them a lesson.

If unknown, non-related dogs are involved, the situation can be quite different, and you cannot count on any protective behaviour towards a puppy, especially, he is older than fourteen to sixteen weeks. If a puppy meets an adult dog who is unknown to him, and is too rude to him, it is be quite possible that the dog may discipline the little chap with a menacing growl, or take a snap at him. This would be completely normal behaviour, and the adult dog is definitely not disturbed, as is often alleged by indignant puppy owners. You must not display any gestures of pity towards your puppy in this situation. The puppy is learning how to interpret the signals he receives from other dogs correctly, and how to behave appropriately as a member of a social structure.

EVERYDAY LIFE WITH THE PUPPY

Species-appropriate play and dealing with puppies properly both promote a close relationship between human and dog. It is important for this relationship that the little chap develops an almost unlimited trust towards his human pack members.

The prerequisite for a harmonious relationship between human and dog is the ability to understand each other. Due to living in close proximity to us humans, dogs quickly learn how to interpret our language correctly – vocal speech as well as body language. Our body posture and facial expression tell them a lot about our mood, and dogs, unlike any other animal, know how to relate to this and respond accordingly. We, too, should make an effort to understand our canine friend's language, to ensure that we can recognise his needs and understand his moods.

Communication

For the dog as a social pack animal, communication is very important. The ancestors living in the wild were only successful if the pack was co-operating as a team. Any living together in a group can only function smoothly if the animals are able to communicate with each other. For example, small gestures or threatening moves are often enough to clarify the pack hierarchy, and they save the bother of having to fight continuous battles to maintain the pecking order. Doing so would mean having to expend valuable energy, and it might also cause injury, which in turn would not just damage the individual, because a pack member becoming incapacitated, but would also weaken the whole pack.

This is why dogs have an extensive repertoire of signals at their disposal, in the area of body language as well as vocal signals. They are, however, not born with

Even the smallest pups know how to signal submission towards higher ranking dogs. (Photo: Widmann)

the ability to master these signals. Although many behaviours are innate and to a certain degree guided by instinct, they only develop over a period of time, as the puppy is growing up. As the puppy is developing physically he has the ability to utter different sounds and display various facial expressions and body language. But he will only be able to learn the meaning of these signals, and how they are employed correctly in the context with his fellow canines, by interacting with other dogs during the socialisation phase. He is already equipped with all the tools for communication, but he has yet to learn how to use them in the proper manner.

This is the reason why puppies who have never had the opportunity to make contact with other dogs in a free and easy manner and to learn proper dog behaviour will have problems later on when coming across fellow adult canines. Occasionally being put into one's place by an older or higher ranking dog for misbehaviour is a normal part of this. This is the only way they can learn the meaning of threatening behaviour and how peace can be restored by displaying the relevant signals for appeasement and submission.

The adult dog has a great repertory of signals at his disposal, which he can use for communication with other dogs and with us. The possibilities for the puppy are still limited, but with each day and during every encounter with other dogs he will learn and expand his linguistic abilities. Many signals and especially body language will only be learnt and used when the dog has reached sexual maturity.

This is also the time when he begins to develop territorial behaviour and a certain amount of posturing. The puppy is able to display some signals, such as those for appeasement or submission, at a relatively early age, in order to protect himself from being attacked by other dogs. In the following the most important 'vocabulary' of dog language are listed, which can already be observed in puppies or young dogs.

Sound language

Whelping – Puppies only make these sounds in the three first weeks of their life, and they signal slight discomfort.

Grumbling – These sounds are only made by puppies and signal greater discomfort. Later they develop into the growl.

Whimpering, yowling or whining – These are sound signals meaning discomfort, unease and sometimes just impatience. They are displayed by puppies, as well as adult dogs. An act of active submission can also be accompanied by whimpering.

Crying – Dogs can cry when they are in a lot of pain or when they had a shock.

Growling – Growling is developed from grumbling and can often be heard during play with humans or dogs. Puppies don't normally growl as an expression of aggression or insecurity yet. It will be used in the relevant situations as they get older.

Barking – Puppies have to learn how to bark. The time at which a puppy barks for the first time can vary quite a lot. Barking has a variety of functions, and it sounds different depending on the situation: alarm, warning, greeting, invitation to play or impatience.

Howling – This is the most primordial sound dogs can make, and will only be heard if a dog has been abandoned and is feeling lonely.

Sighing – This sound is a sign of well-being, and will be uttered when the dog is in a state of total relaxation, usually just before dropping off to sleep.

Facial expression and body language

Lip licking – Puppies nudge and lick their mother around the mouth area in order to encourage her to regurgitate some morsels of food after she has returned from hunting. This behaviour has been ritualised and serves as a gesture of submission.

Jumping up – Puppies and also many grown-up dogs like to jump up against us as a greeting. They just want to get close to our faces in order to be able to carry out the lip-licking as a ritualised begging gesture.

Handshake – This is a gesture of appeasement that a lower ranking dog displays towards a dominant dog. Towards a human, it is displayed as an invitation to play or as a begging gesture.

Bowing – The low front body position with the posterior pointing upwards can be observed in young puppies and it means an invitation to play.

Yawning –
This is almost always a calming signal as a sign of insecurity or as appeasement.
Lying on back – this is the most direct way of showing submission. Puppies in particular use it to appease other dogs and us humans, often producing a little urine too. Don't scold your dog for this, as this would only make matters worse. With increasing age and confidence, the submissive urinating will stop by itself.

The nudging of the mouth area is a ritualised lip licking gesture and is used for appeasement. (Photo: Lehari)

Ears pinned back –This gesture, often in combination with a pulling back of the lips, is a gesture of submission that the adult dog will carry on doing. The dog tries to make himself smaller in order to demonstrate how harmless he is.

61

Puppies like to sleep tightly cuddled up to each other. (Photo: Widmann)

Cuddling up

Physical contact is very important for a dog, and above all for a puppy. If you observe a pack of wolves or dogs, you will notice that the animals will try and get into close physical contact with each other, especially during quiet periods. This is done to the point where one dog literally squeezes in between the others, so they end up lying almost on top of each other, and then go to sleep

in this position. You must not prevent your puppy from having this close physical contact. The best time for this is in the evening when the little chap is settling down for the night, full, tired and happy. Take him on your lap, or have him lie next to you, or on your tummy, and enjoy the trust that your puppy shows towards you when he ends up falling asleep snuggled up against you. If you

Cuddling up is important for a close and trusting relationship. (Photo: Lehari)

don't want your dog to lie next to you on the sofa, lie down next to him on the carpet for a while, in order to give him the opportunity to feel in close physical contact with you.

You should start cuddling up to your puppy from the first day onwards, because it contributes tremendously to the development of a close bond and the feeling of mutual trust between human and dog. Whilst cuddling up to him, you can also get your puppy used to being turned on his back and being touched on various parts of his body, by stroking him gently all over. This can be quite useful with a view to future veterinary exams and treatments for example. A dog who completely trusts his human will be more prepared to endure slightly unpleasant procedures than a distrustful dog, who may even have had bad experiences in the past.

The biting inhibition has to be practised until the little pup has learnt to be more gentle when playing with his partner. (Photo: Widmann)

Biting inhibition

It has been assumed in the past that the biting inhibition was innate. Today it is known that this too has to be learnt, and the best time for this is the time before the milk teeth are exchanged for adult teeth. Begin practising this already within the first minutes of time spent together with your dog. Every time he bites you firmly, let off a screaming 'Ouch' or a clear 'No', while at the same time turning away from him. The puppy will realise very soon that being bitten by his pointy little teeth is not very funny.

Dogs behave like this too, when they are amongst themselves. They give off a loud whine and ignore the aggressive play-mate, if he were to treat them too roughly. But because it isn't in the ruffian's interest to break off the game, he will be more careful in the future about how he uses his teeth. If the boisterous little tyke doesn't let go in response to your wailing, then you can briefly and determinedly put your hand around his snout from above. But don't hold his little mouth shut for any prolonged period of time. The idea of using the snout grip, or dominance grip originated from watching the behaviour of dog-like animals amongst each other. Dog parents use it for disciplining their offspring when they misbehave.

The snout grip can also be used if the little rascal has got something in his mouth and doesn't want to let go, or if he is holding on to it with grim determination. A dog has to learn to let go with objects, or even food, when he is asked to. The snout grip involves putting your thumb as well as your index and middle finger over the puppy's snout and pressing more or less hard (depending on the resistance offered) on both sides of the upper jaw. He will subsequently open his mouth. Make sure that you're always the winner in this exercise, otherwise the little pup will have already managed to call your dominance into question.

After a short break turn back to the puppy, and in a friendly manner invite him to continue playing. If he remains adequately affectionate, praise him adequately. By this behaviour you are teaching him a number of important lessons: namely, that biting and nipping does not get him attention, and that you alone are boss and give the command to begin, continue or end an undertaking.

By the way, the feeding of treats (not meals) from the hand also reinforces the biting inhibition, because the puppy learns how to interact gently with a human hand.

All exercises regarding discipline involve reinforcing the desired behaviour by giving praise and/or a treat, while ignoring undesired behaviour. It is immeasurably worse for the little pup to be ignored, rather than being scolded or physically chastised after a transgression, because doing this means you are dealing with him, which the puppy may interpret as giving him attention and thus providing positive reinforcement.

Proper play

As described in the context of the biting inhibition, it is a matter for the pack leader to initiate and to end a playing session. This helps reinforce the pecking order, and the little pup learns in a playful manner who is boss, and who gets to make the decisions. Of course, you can occasionally allow yourself to become involved in playing when your puppy comes running to you with his favourite squeaky toy. But always remember to end the session halfway through, and to be the one who initiates the next session. If the puppy becomes too boisterous or overexcited during play, you must end the playing session and ignore him for a while. If he won't leave you alone, just walk away. He will calm down quickly and probably fall asleep in his basket soon after. You can then initiate another playing session later.

In order for the young dog to learn right from the start which objects he is allowed to play with, from day one he should be given toys that belong to him alone. Generally, anything is suitable that cannot be swallowed or bitten to pieces by the dog, or anything that in not any way dangerous to him. It is best to buy special dog toys

You can already practise proper fetching during play using a puppy's dummy. (Photo: Widmann)

that have been created with the dog's needs in mind, and made of a material able to withstand a dog's teeth. Squeaky toys are a particular favourite. As soon as the dog has worked out how to get a squeaky noise out of his toy by judiciously applying pressure, he will enthusiastically carry it about the house whilst moving his jaws rhythmically, thus producing rhythmic squeaks. Many a dog owner will be glad if the toy turns out not to be able to withstand this level of use after all, and loses its squeak at some point because it has sprung a hole. However, dogs who have a pronounced preying instinct should only play with 'dumb' toys, because it is possible that the biting inhibition, triggered by the 'victim's' screams and yowls cannot develop properly, because the toy does not appear to be suffering any damage despite the squeaking. If you notice the dog is playing too violently with a toy, take it away from him and offer him a different one. This is type of toy isn't recommended either for dogs who are trained for fetching and who are supposed to keep their mouth 'gentle', because they get into the habit of mauling the prey, i.e., biting into it too hard.

Also popular are balls or 'kong' dog toys, which have a rope attached to them, or knots made from sturdy rope, available in various sizes. Make sure they are well made and don't easily lose fibres that could be swallowed by the puppy. All these toys can be thrown or used to play tug-of-war, but you must bear in mind two things: don't pull too hard, otherwise there is a risk of teeth being pulled out by force, especially during the change from milk teeth to adult teeth; and puppies who display dominant or even aggressive behaviour early on should not be encouraged to play tug – of-war games, because they work up too much of a frenzy otherwise. If you are dealing with a timid or insecure puppy on the other hand, you can have a good pull with him, while letting the puppy win every so often, because this will strengthen his confidence.

The pecking order

Normally, puppies have no problem accepting that they are at the bottom of the pecking order, and that they have to follow our instructions. There are some dogs, however, who will display extremely dominant behaviour even as puppies. They will, for example, find it difficult to learn the biting inhibition, or constantly try to ride up your leg. One effective countermeasure is to turn the puppy on his back. For this, you grip the puppy by the scruff of his neck and push him on his back, accompanied by strict words. You do this as long as it takes (!) until he puts his tail between his legs in the direction of his tummy, indicating submission. The longer it takes, the more dominant he is. This dominance shown already in the puppy must not be underestimated, because at some point the dog will grow up and then he will try

to tyrannise you. Turning the puppy on his back should be practised during play every now and again, in order to confirm the pecking order.

Rules for dealing with a dominant puppy

- Do not react to any invitations to play coming from the puppy; always be the one who determines when and for how long the playing session should last
- Always be the first to walk through a narrow passage (a doorway, for example)
- Make the puppy wait for his food until you give him permission
- Be consistent
- Don't ever ask him to do something that cannot be enforced
- Don't allow the puppy in your bed
- Don't play tug-of-war with him, as this will encourage his potential fighting instincts
- Always show him who's boss

If your puppy shows no sign of dominating behaviour and fits in well into his position within the pack, you can of course relax some of these rules.

PUPPY EDUCATION –

THE FIRST LESSONS

Even if your dog is purely a family and companion dog, he should show at least a basic level of obedience, as well as mastering the most important lessons. This is the only way to guarantee that he will reliably react to your commands, that he will behave nicely towards other humans and animals and that consequently you will be able to take him almost anywhere. The amount of freedom a dog is able to enjoy is directly linked to his ability to be obedient.

Dogs learn best by positive reinforcement. This is based on the experience that behaviours that are associated with pleasure, such as a treat, are displayed more often than those that don't prompt any reaction, or that result in unpleasant events, such as the withdrawal of attention. With the help of treats you are not only able to reward puppy, but you can also get him to do certain things. In order to do this, you lure the little chap with a treat, for example to establish eye contact with you, or to have him walk next to you.

You cannot start early enough with the basic training, because the puppy's tremendous ability to absorb, especially during the socialisation phase, and he'll learn the most important lessons almost effortlessly whilst playing. If you attend a puppy group, you will carry out the first exercises there. These and additional exercises can be practised and reinforced at home with your puppy every day. However, don't practise for too long, because a puppy can only concentrate for very short periods of time. With increasing age, the practice time can be extended from a few minutes to longer sessions.

The puppy has to concentrate on you for each exercise. Don't start the lesson unless he has established eye contact with you. You can get the puppy in the mood and get his attention for the exercise with the help of a game or a treat. As soon a you notice that the pupil's concentration is waning, conclude the lesson with an exercise

With a lot of praise and treats as positive reinforcements, the puppy will learn quickly, concentrate more and view the exercises as a pleasant experience. (Photo: Lehari)

that you know will definitely work well. Then you can praise your puppy heartily, and let him scamper about freely or play with him. An experience of success at the end motivates the dog, and guarantees his undivided attention and enthusiasm the next time round. Once he has learnt all the lessons regarding basic obedience, they have to be practised regularly, preferably daily, so they are not forgotten again, but instead become ingrained into every fibre of the dog's being.

The important thing with all these exercises is that the reward must be given instantly, i.e., within two seconds of the exercise being carried out correctly. This is the only way that the puppy will be able to associate the reward with having carried out the exercise. It is always the puppy's last action that he will associate with the praise or the treat. This is why the learning success also depends on the correct timing by the human. Undesired behaviour or wrongly executed exercises should be ignored. This way the puppy learns that it's only worth his while if he concentrates on carrying out the exercises correctly. Even admonishing or scolding him when puppy has done something wrong may be seen by him as a form of positive attention and thus as a reward, thereby reinforcing the wrong behaviour. This is why it's best to ignore any undesirable behaviour.

If the puppy associates coming to you with something pleasant, he'll come running with flying ears. (Photo: Widmann)

Recall

When called, a dog has to come to his human without fail. This, of course, also has to involve reacting to his name, which is best accompanied by the word 'come'. These exercises can be carried out with the puppy right from the start. As soon as he moves in your direction, call his name accompanied by 'come' and then praise him heartily. He will soon react to his name and will come when called. You'll have give him generous praise

every time. This can be done by giving him a good cuddle, a game or a tasty treat. Whatever you settle on, the puppy must always associate coming to you with something pleasant.

You can even exploit the daily feeding sessions for training purposes. Have the puppy wait in another room while the food is being prepared, or prepare the food while he is busy doing something else or is otherwise distracted. Put the food bowl in the usual spot and call the puppy. He will have learnt this lesson in a very short

A puppy can only be recalled from playing with other dogs if he has already formed a close bond with his human, and if the human is interesting to him. (Photo: Steimer)

time and will come running instantly when you call him. If you want to train your dog to react to acoustic signals, for example a retriever whistle, you can start using this for recall training straightaway. The recall whistle (usually a short double whistle) replaces the word used for recall.

After a while, the training can be carried out at greater intervals and also out of doors. Even if he is taking his time, you still have to praise him if he has reacted to the command 'Come'. Don't be tempted to scold him if you think he isn't coming to you fast enough, or if he has run off and only reappears after a longer period of time. The last action – in this case coming to you – has to be rewarded. A dog would not understand a punishment for something that has happened before. He will associate it with his last action (coming to you), and would, of course, feel less and less inclined to obey your command if he felt he was being punished for it.

While you are outdoors or out walking, and your puppy is very distracted playing with other dogs or something else, don't call him, because in all probability he will not react. This is normal in puppies and has nothing to do with disobedience. They simply become so wrapped up in their play that at this moment in time this is the most important thing in the world. As they get older, dogs will increasingly concentrate on their human, and can be recalled from this kind of situation.

So, if your little rascal doesn't react to you, just go to him without saying anything, put him on the leash and take him with you. If he goes with you like a good dog and pays attention to you, naturally you have to praise him straightaway. You should behave in the same manner whilst attending the puppy group. If your puppy is still too young to be recalled from the play with others, put him on the leash without saying anything, instead of calling him again and again. Otherwise he'll only learn that frequent calling is something to be ignored.

Only practise this once the little chap is concentrating on you. In this situation he should come to you imme-

diately after being called once, or twice at the most. If that doesn't work, go back to practising in the house and make yourself interesting to the puppy. It is also important that you should call him in a cheerful, even enthusiastic manner, because this mood will immediately transfer to the puppy, even if neighbours or passers-by may give you strange looks at times. The main thing is that your dog enjoys coming to you.

In the first few weeks, a puppy generally stays close to his human, and will instantly run after him, as soon as the human is walking in the opposite direction. As he gets older, the little chap becomes increasingly confident and will occasionally embark on a little excursion by himself. If he has not yet learnt the 'come' command reliably by then, or suddenly doesn't react to being called any more, you can practise by attaching a thin piece of tow string about ten metres long to the puppy's collar, and then you simply leave it to drag across the ground. As soon as the puppy gets too far away, you step on

the string, causing him to stop in his tracks with a jolt. He will at first be startled about how far your 'arm' can reach. Call him to come to you and reward him immediately as soon he has arrived. Afterwards let him run off again. After a while he will learn not to go any further than this imaginary border, making the tow string superfluous.

Whatever you do, don't make the mistake of running after the puppy, if he refuses to come and trying to escape your influence. The puppy will see this as a diverting game, especially because he will soon realise that you have no chance of catching him. Turn round and run in the opposite direction. The puppy will be baffled and stop. In the end he will come after you because, after all, he won't want to lose contact with his pack. Once he has caught up with you, show him how exceedingly pleased you are and reward him with a game or a tasty treat.

A good way for the dog to practise the recall, which you can always incorporate in you daily walks at a later stage as well, is playing hide-and-seek. Later on, the adult dog should follow your example, always paying attention to what you're up to and which direction you're taking. If the puppy has put too much distance between himself and you and doesn't pay any attention to you any more, quickly hide behind a tree or a fence (only do this exercise away from busy streets). At some point the puppy will turn round and look for you. As you have now disappeared from view all of a sudden, he will retrace his steps and search for you, having to use his nose for this purpose as well. If he has difficulties locating you, call him quietly, once he is getting close to you. You will find that he'll be beside himself with joy, and for a while afterwards he'll be keeping an extra close eye on you. But don't do this exercise too often, otherwise the effect quickly wears off. The hide-and-seek exercise is neither necessary nor appropriate if you are dealing with a nervous or insecure puppy.

Getting used to collar or harness usually doesn't take long at all. (Photo: Widmann)

Getting used to collar and leash

It is a good idea to put the collar or harness on your puppy from the first day onwards; do this when he is distracted while eating or playing. This way he will quickly get used to wearing this unfamiliar item. Divert his attention whenever he tries to scratch on it. Once the puppy has got used to the collar, attach a thin, light leash to it – even inside the house – which can trail behind him. Take the end of the leash and walk behind the puppy in such a manner that the leash is never tightened. The puppy should not experience the leash as a constriction. Coax him with kind words and a treat towards you, without pulling on the leash, and reward him appropriately. You can soon take him outside on the leash, too, but at the beginning avoid pulling on it.

Leash training and walking to heel

A dog should be able to walk to heel without any problem both on a leash and without it. The correct walking to heel position is on the left side (the dog should also walk on your left side if you are on a bicycle, away from the traffic). As soon as the puppy has got used to leash and collar, you can start with the training – only for a short period each time – first in the house and garden, and later outside, too. Don't allow the puppy to play with the leash, bite into it and pull on it; he can use other toys for this. When he accidentally comes to walk on you left side, without pulling on the leash say the command 'Heel' and praise him heartily. Just ignore all other behaviour.

After a few days, the puppy will have understood the point of the exercise. Now you can start to correct his mistakes. If he doesn't want to come with you, don't pull him behind you, but instead beckon him to follow. If he pulls forward, just stop without saying anything, until he comes back to you. Give him the command 'Heel' and praise him once he is walking next to you properly. If he dashes forward again, repeat this game. Soon the little tearaway will get bored with having to stop all the time, and rather walk by your side like a good dog. Depending on the dog's temperament, however, it can take some time to achieve enduring learning success. The person in charge of the dog will have to be very patient, even if the walk has to be interrupted on numerous occasions. A treat, held in such a way that the puppy can see it, can be very helpful with this. He will look up to you in eager anticipation of the treat, while obligingly walking next to you. After a short while reward him with the treat.

Always conclude the training unit on a successful note; in other words, when the puppy has been walking to heel

Walking to heel should only ever be practised for a short period of time, because a puppy can't yet concentrate for very long. (Photo: Steimer)

properly, reward him with a final treat before taking off his leash and playing with him. This way he will also learn to distinguish between leisure and work.

According to experience, this gentle method is at least as successful as the method of giving the leash a short sharp pull, which is often recommended. This will work with sensitive dogs, but these tend to react very quickly to other methods as well, and therefore don't need such treatment anyway. In contrast, agile and lively dogs will usually be less than impressed with the short sharp pull method, because their well-developed neck muscles make them quite insensitive to it, and it may encourage them to pull on the leash even more.

Once the puppy has learnt to walk on the leash properly, the next exercise is for the dog to follow freely. As the dog already knows the command 'heel' already, he will know what you're asking of him even without a leash. Of course, an extra amount of praise is now required once more, and this exercise, too, should only be done for a few seconds at a time, and maybe two to three minutes later on, because a young dog isn't able to concentrate on walking to heel for any longer than that.

If the dog moves a little distance away from you, stop and call his name accompanied by 'Come'. As soon as he is next to you, give the command 'Heel' and praise him if he is behaving correctly. Don't praise him too enthusiastically, though, because he might interpret this as an invitation to dash away or to play. The free walking to heel requires a lot of discipline and practice. Only once the free walking to heel works really well can you start practising this with any distractions happening around you, such as a passing pedestrian, a cyclist or – and this must be the hardest one to resist – another dog. The amount of time it will take until the dog is able to walk to heel freely depends on the dog's individual disposition and breed. You cannot expect this of a puppy.

'Sit' and 'down'

Every puppy is able to sit and to lie down. Hence you can practise 'sit' and 'down' in a playful manner and with a treat as a reward right from the beginning.

Most puppies will learn quite quickly how to sit on command. Sit or stand in front of the puppy and hold a treat above his head, Once he realises that he won't be able to reach it easily, he will sit down soon enough. Quickly give him the command 'Sit', praise him and pass him his well-earned treat. The dog will quickly realise what this command involves. At the same time, you can point upwards the first digit of the hand containing the treat, thereby combining this commonly used visual signal for 'sit' with the acoustic signal. Soon the puppy will sit down in anticipation of his reward prompted by only the visual signal.

The 'sit' can be practised with the puppy right from the beginning. (Photo: Steimer)

This exercise can be repeated every so often at all possible occasions: before feeding, before play or before putting the leash on. The command 'Sit' will soon become so ingrained that it won't be necessary any more to reward the puppy with a treat every time.

On the other hand, lying down on command is considerably harder. Because the dog is even further away from our face when he is flat on the ground, and because it is harder to jump up quickly or run away from this position than it is from the 'sit' position, it is difficult to get him to comply, especially when this lesson is practised from scratch. After he has got into the lying down position at long last, the dog will often jump up again like a coiled spring as soon as the first word of praise

The command 'down' requires a little more practice and concentration. Photo: Steimer)

is uttered. Very wilful puppies in particular will require a lot of discipline for this exercise.

Have the dog stand or sit in front of you and move your hand (containing a treat) around, just above the ground in front of him. He will, of course, try to get to the treat. If he finally lies down, give him the command 'Down' and reward him with the treat from your hand straightaway. As soon as the puppy has understood that the command 'down' means lying down, only give him a hand signal by pointing towards the ground with an open palm, and without holding a treat in your hand. The reward will only be given after the exercise has been successfully completed. From this the dog will also learn to obey visual as well as acoustic signals.

'No' can be used in many different ways, always when the puppy does something he's not supposed to. (Photo: Steimer)

'No'

One of the most important commands, which should be practised as early as possible and which can be vital in certain circumstances, is the word 'no'. It means: no matter what you are doing right now or what you are about to do, stop it! This can involve gnawing on carpet fringes or chair legs, digging in the garden, chasing cats or other animals, biting too hard during play, and many more things.

Teaching the meaning of the word 'no' cannot be started early enough. As soon as the puppy has moved into his new home and begins carrying out undesired actions,

such as gnawing on a shoe, you immediately say 'No' in a strict tone of voice, while you pick up the little chap and put him down somewhere else. Then you divert his attention with a toy or a chew bone. If he busies himself with that, praise him heartily. As soon as he does anything forbidden, he is reprimanded with a 'No', and has his attention diverted to something else once more. It is known from experience that dogs very quickly understand the meaning of the word 'no', soon making it sufficient to just say the command, in order to prevent him from engaging in a particular action.

What is important above all is that the reprimand regarding a forbidden action follows immediately after the act has been perpetrated. A punishment for something that has happened several minutes – or even hours – ago is completely pointless. The dog cannot make the connection between the act and the punishment, and will react to it with a total lack of understanding, or he will associate the punishment with the most recent action.

If the puppy has understood the meaning of the word 'no' already, the most effective way of using it is at the point when he is about to do something undesirable. His human, having observed him and thus realised what he is planning to do, can now nip the dog's intention in the bud with a timely 'No'. If you're used to observing your puppy closely, you will notice the tension and his intentions immediately from his body language. A timely 'No' followed by another command such as 'Come', 'Heel' or 'Sit' (if he has already learnt their meaning) and, of course, hearty praise upon obeying it, will turn the previous undesirable intention around into a positive experience for the dog, provided he is obedient. This way you can achieve a great learning success.

The puppy will also be very impressed if he can't see you while he is about to do something naughty, as you're watching him from some hiding place, you can let off a strict 'No' at just the right moment. He will be baffled and stop his action, and he will, at least for a while, be convinced of your omnipotence and omnipresence.

However, you won't always be able to read your dog's mind in time for intervention. Once he has gone some distance away from his human, it will be more and more difficult to stop him from doing something you don't want him to. In these cases, it can help to throw a rattling object after the dog. This could be a bunch of keys, a throw chain or something similar. Surprised by the long arm of the human as the projectile lands with a loud rattling noise on the ground next to him, the puppy will return immediately. This ought to be followed by some enthusiastic praise and a treat. After having used the rattling projectile a few times, it will be sufficient later just to rattle the object in order to persuade the little chap to forego certain undesired actions. This method is very useful, for example, in order to break the habit of chasing cyclists, joggers, cars, etc., something that hunting dogs tend to be very fond of doing. Enlisting the help of an assistant who can pose as a passing cyclist or jogger would be perfect for this, because this way you can practise the correct behaviour more pointedly. If the dog carries on walking to heel despite the distraction, ample praise is in order, as well as a particularly tasty treat.

Once the puppy has learnt to be on his own, he'll spend most of the waiting time asleep. (Photo: Widmann)

Home alone

Because there are always be situations where a dog isn't able to accompany his humans, he will have to learn to be on his own as soon as possible. Once you take a puppy into your house and he has settled into his new home, you should start training.

The best time to start is when the puppy is tired after having eaten, played and been outside to do his business. Put him in his basket or transport crate, put a toy and a chew bone inside with him, so he has something to do. Stroke him and then quietly leave the room. If the dog is not used to a transport crate that can be closed, you should only leave him on his own in a room where he can't do much damage. The hall of a flat, for instance, is only a good place for him if all the family members' shoes aren't lined up on the floor there; shoes make wonderful objects for chewing. All kinds of items of clothing, towels or paper hankies are welcome objects for passing the time, if they are within the puppy's reach.

Don't leave the puppy alone for more than a few minutes to begin with. If he has been quiet, return to him and praise him. If he becomes anxious and yowls or whimpers, and hasn't calmed down within a very short period of time, distract him by making a sound, so he briefly goes quiet. Go to him and, if necessary, put him back into his basket and stroke him. Then leave the room again immediately, and if he stays quiet, go back to him after a short moment in order to praise him. It is important that the puppy associates the praise with his quiet behaviour. It is essential not to punish him for the wrong reason.

It is normally quite easy to get a puppy used to staying in on his own. As soon as he has realised that he isn't being abandoned and that you'll always come back, he will stop being scared and wait for his human to return, all relaxed and full of trust. Dogs who have learnt to be on their own usually spend most of the waiting time asleep anyway.

The length of time during which the puppy is left to stay on his own can gradually be extended. In order to be sure that the dog really does remain quiet whilst on his own, you could have a tape recorder recording any environmental noises while you're out, or you could spend some time at your neighbour's in order to be able to hear what's going on from there. If it turns out your dog is making noise for the whole duration, you'll have to go back to training him to stay on his own for shorter periods of time.

If your puppy hasn't had to learn how to be on his own early in life, it will take a lot more energy and patience to get the dog used to being on his own. Some dogs get so anxious and scared when being left alone that they will not eat while their humans are absent, and will instead scratch and bite doors, windows and walls or other objects in an attempt to follow their pack members.

One mistake that is often made when dealing with anxious dogs is to conduct exaggerated farewell and welcoming ceremonies. A dog is instantly aware when you are getting ready to go out. If you then make a big fuss over saying goodbye to him, and telling him that he need not be scared, a dog who is already nervous will become even more anxious and exasperated. The best way to deal with this is to not pay any attention to him during the last quarter of an hour before you leave. Behave as if you going out is the most normal thing in the world, and don't turn it into a ceremony.

Try to distract the dog with a chew bone before going out, so that he is occupied the whole time. Once he is chewing on the bone, just leave without saying a word. If your dog stays quiet for a while due to this diversion, you may, as described above, return and praise his good behaviour. The more often you practise going out, the sooner you'll achieve a learning success.

At the beginning the puppy should always associate a car ride with something positive. (Photo: Widmann)

Car rides

Puppies normally love travelling by car, because they enjoy being part of everything. At the beginning, only take your puppy on short car journeys, which he will experience as something positive. The first trip should not necessarily be the trip to the vet. Drive to a nearby meadow and allow your little charge to run around for a bit and relieve himself, and play with him for a while, or drive to a meeting point to join other dog owners, in order to allow your pup to play with other dogs, which will ensure he'll associate car rides with a nice adventure. Afterwards, drive back home.

If your puppy still doesn't like travelling in a car, feed him inside the stationary car for a while with the engine turned off. After a few times, you can let the engine run while feeding him and talking to him in a soothing voice. If this works without problem, your next car journeys should be more successful.

Puppies who don't like travelling by car should be prevented from looking out of the windows during the journey. Looking at the fast-moving landscape may make them nauseous. If this is the case the puppy should not be given the opportunity to look out of the window, or moreover to clamber around the inside of the car (not advisable due to security reasons, anyway). During an emergency stop or an accident, an unsecured dog can cause injury or even death to himself or, for that matter, his human fellow passengers, too, or he may even be the cause of the accident in the first place. That's why it is best to secure dogs with a special harness, to confine them to a part of the car that is separated by a grille, or to put them in a special crate.

Should car rides still not agree with the puppy after all these efforts, consult the vet. Sometimes there may be a physical problem that may cause the puppy to feel unwell. These can be helped with medicines, Bach flowers, homeopathic remedies or special massage.

THE PUPPY IN A FAMILY SITUATION

The puppy and children

The experiences that the little pup has had with children determine to a large degree how the adult dog will behave towards children in the future. Many breed descriptions mark certain breeds out as particularly child friendly. In my view, however, there is a risk that this may lead to parents who have no previous experience with dogs to rely too much on such descriptions. They may end up believing that their puppy is the ideal playmate for their children without the necessity for any contribution on their part. Whether or not or in what way a puppy or adult dog is going to be child friendly is less dependent on the breed, but rather on the environment in which he has grown up, how he was socialised and what experiences he has had. There certainly are dog breeds that have a higher stimulus threshold than others and who will be more indulgent towards small children, but this does not absolve you from all responsibility.

Once children have learnt how to treat a dog properly, they make a good team. (Photo: Widmann)

There are two prerequisites for children and dogs getting on with each other harmoniously: the children have to learn how to treat dogs properly as early as possible; and the dogs should be given the opportunity to have good experiences with children during the imprinting phase in their puppyhood, and should be brought up in such a way that they don't pose any risk to children, whether they are other people's children or those of the dog's own family pack. In some situations it is advisable to put the puppy in an indoor kennel where he is safe from children, and unable to do much damage either. It has been the suggested that a puppy won't put a pre-pubescent child on a par with an adult, but instead will perceive him as a puppy and not accept him as superior in the pecking order.

Parents should explain to their children as soon as possible how to behave correctly towards a dog, be it a puppy or an adult dog.

Here are some of the most important rules:

- *Don't touch the dog on the head from above; it's better to stroke him on his chest or ears*
- *Don't pull the dog's tail or ears, or poke him in the eyes or nostrils.*
- *Don't approach the dog from behind and startle him.*
- *Don't push the dog into a corner.*
- *Don't disturb the dog while he's eating or sleeping.*
- *Don't scream loudly, or run away screaming.*
- *Don't blow on the dog.*
- *Leave the dog alone when he turns away or growls.*
- *Don't leave any toys lying around or they may be chewed or swallowed.*

A child should not give training commands to the dog, because he would not be able to enforce them.

Experience has shown that children learn very quickly how to deal with dogs properly, if they are taught the right way by adults. If the puppy has had positive experiences dealing with children he will become a dependable playmate. Should he be too boisterous during play and bite too hard, he has to be reprimanded by an adult. The pointy milk teeth can be quite painful, and may quickly cause tears (see the section 'Biting inhibition' in the chapter 'Imprinting and socialisation'). Equally, he must not ride up on the child or steal food from him. If the puppy has understood the basic rules, it is very likely that he will grow up in harmony with children and become a faithful friend to them later on.

Small children and puppies should never be left alone together unsupervised, even when every kind of safeguard is in place, because both can be quite boisterous, and their behaviour isn't entirely predictable. Therefore you can never be sure that things won't go wrong.

The puppy and other animals

A puppy is completely naïve as far as anything new and unknown is concerned, and he will also approach any other animal without fear. That's why the puppy stage is the best time to get the little chap acquainted with a large variety of representatives of other species, as already mentioned in the chapter 'Imprinting and socialisation'. Taking the little pup to a farm on a regular basis is a good way to go about it, or you can take him for walks in a rural area, so he'll get to know chickens and ducks, cows and pigs, sheep and goats, horses and donkeys, for example. If the dog is first confronted with large animals only as an adult, he may react to them with fear and flight, and regard smaller animals such as fowl or rabbits as prey. Passionate herding dogs will often attempt to herd animals on pastures and paddocks, which can be a risk to all concerned – and which the cattle owners won't be too pleased about either. If, on the other hand, the dog is familiar with these animals from the beginning, you'll save yourself a lot of hassle and stress, rather than having to try and undo the dog's bad habits at a later stage. For this reason, dogs who have grown up on farms or at riding stables will usually behave in a more friendly way towards other animals, or at least ignore them.

If a puppy arrives in a household where other pets are being cared for already, such as guinea pigs, rabbits, cats, birds and other small animals, he has to be brought into supervised contact with these animals to ensure that he'll get used to them and leave them alone. Animals kept in cages should be left in their safe abode to begin with, so that the puppy can watch them at his leisure whilst getting used to their smell and way of moving. Dogs normally learn quite quickly who is part of the family and therefore not to be considered prey. But as long as the little rascal is still too boisterous, and there is a risk

Ideally, the puppy should get used to other animal species from an early age. (Photo: Lehari)

that he'll chase the other animals and possibly even grab them with his pointy teeth, those animals always have to be kept in their protective cages when the dog is present. The same applies later on regarding free-roaming pets or free-flying birds; they should not be left unsupervised in the same room with the dog.

If there is a cat already living in the household, he will probably be less than enthusiastic about the presence of the little monster at first. Don't force the cat to come into contact with the puppy. Upon their first meeting, the cat will probably watch the newcomer from the safety of

a lofty place. The puppy will, of course, see the cat as a welcome playmate, and probably try to make a dash towards her straightaway. The amount of time it takes for the cat to establish contact with the puppy on her own initiative, or at least no longer run away from him, can vary, depending on whether the cat is familiar with dogs already or how steady her nerves are. In this situation, too, you should never leave the two of them together unsupervised, because a cat can defend himself very effectively. If possible, you should prevent the puppy from having a bad experience with this species, because of the risk he might turn into a cat-hater. There are many examples, however, to prove that cats and dogs can get used to each other quite quickly, and live harmoniously under the same roof. In this situation, it is important that the humans invest a lot of time into their charges, and give the cat as much attention as she used to get before, in order to prevent her from feeling second best and associating this with the presence of the puppy. Once again, a tasty treat rewarding good behaviour ensures a desirable result.

The puppy as a second dog

Generally, it can be said that keeping two or more dogs in a household is more species-appropriate than keeping a single dog on his own. Due to the long period of domestication, however, our dogs have adapted to the needs of their human pack members and they are not suffering unduly if there isn't always another dog near them. But people who can afford the space, the time and the money, and like a lot hurly-burly around them – because keeping two dogs is far more demanding than keeping just one – will often consider getting a second dog.

Even if a dog is very attached to his humans and has his firm place in the family pack, he will usually still enjoy having contact with another dog. This already becomes obvious upon observing the great interest that dogs tend to have for other dogs that they meet while out walking. With another dog, he can scamper about and play as rumbustiously as dogs do, because a dog is not as delicate as a human by half; after all, a human is not even in possession of any fur to protect him during boisterous play! Also, if a dog is left on his own, be it in the house or in the garden, a second dog will provide diversion and ward off boredom. They can play together, dig holes, quarrel over a toy or a bone, or simply doze in the sunshine together.

Some people are concerned that dogs who are not kept on their own may be less likely to form a close bond with humans. This isn't true as long as the human is considered to be the pack leader and has enough time to spend with the dogs. Even if several dogs are kept together, they aren't quite happy if they only have each other for company. They demand attention and affection from their human just as much as single dogs do. You should therefore not get a second dog in the hope that this way you'll have to give them less time and attention.

Sooner or later the older dog will allow himself to be roped into playing with the puppy, and consider him as his protégé from that moment onwards, even if the little tyke may be a little rough at times. (Photo: Lehari)

An ideal constellation is to pair off a puppy with an older more experienced dog. The little pup will worship his big friend with enthusiasm, and emulate him in everything. As a result he will be much easier to train, because he will copy such a lot from his older and more experienced role model. A note of caution, though: he will, of course, copy any undesirable behaviour just as much as any desirable behaviour. Therefore you've got to make sure the older dog is a shining example.

Don't worry if the older dog refuses to acknowledge the puppy's existence and ignores him. According to experience, this situation will only last a few days, or a few weeks at the most. This is because the puppy will not relent in his attempts to gain the older dog's attention and to persuade him to play. Finally, the ice is broken, which you will be able to deduce from the fact that both dogs are playing with each other intensively and boisterously.

The puppy is now accepted as a new pack member, and the two dogs will be inseparable from that moment onwards.

On the other hand, getting two puppies at the same time is not advisable. Keeping one little rascal under control and training him is hard enough. If you have two puppies there is a relatively great risk that the two of them will evade your influence altogether, and rather fool around with each other instead of concentrating on the upcoming lessons. In addition, together they will, of course, feel stronger and therefore create much more havoc. Another difficulty is upon visiting the puppy group, where the puppies are, among other things, supposed to learn to concentrate on their human. Perhaps the best way of bringing up two puppies simultaneously would be, if each had his 'own' human, and if each person could from time to time have one of the puppies on a one-to-one basis, and do some training exercises without the other puppy being present.

Finally, a few thoughts on the subject of purchasing a puppy as a replacement for an old dog or a dog who has died. Many dog owners who have lost a dog due to illness or old age at first don't like to even consider getting a new dog. They need a certain period of time for grieving and working through their grief, until they are ready for a new four-legged companion. Others may already think about the next dog, once the present dog has reached a certain age, and wonder whether they can burden their old dog with a whirlwind puppy. From experience it can be said that a puppy is like a elixir of youth for an old dog, provided that he isn't suffering from any major physical frailty yet. Even if the older dog spends most of his day asleep and isn't as interested in all the various activities as he used to be, he will be encouraged by the newcomer to take part in everyday life activities once more. Suddenly he has to defend his food or his favourite spot against this uncouth oaf. In addition, the master or mistress is going outside a lot more often with the little chap – a welcome opportunity to check the scent marks in one's territory a little more frequently again; and if this midget keeps annoying you or tries to rope you into playing with him, there's nothing to be done about it other than joining in and enforcing some discipline as well, while you're at it. A puppy will cause an older dog to become considerably more active. If you give him as much affection as you used to before, he will not feel disadvantaged and will consider the puppy to be his personal protégé.

By the time when finally the day comes for the old dog to go, the little pup will have grown into a fully fledged dog with a firm character, whose presence will make the time of grief and loss a little easier for us.

What does fate have in store for these three rascals?
(Photo: Widmann)

FURTHER READING

Brigitte Rauth-Widmann
Your Dog's Senses
Cadmos Books, 2006

Christina Sondermann
Playtime for your Dog
Cadmos Books, 2006

Anders Hallgren
Mental Activation
Cadmos Books, 2007

Christiane Liebeck
Man-trailing
Cadmos Books, 2008

Manuela Zaitz
Trick School for Dogs
Cadmos Books, 2008

Uli Köppel
The Pack Concept
Cadmos Books, 2008

INDEX